T0340665

INDUSTRIAL RELATIONS: CHALLENGES AND RESPONSES

Edited by JOHN H. G. CRISPO

Industrial relations, which in the past have focused almost entirely on union-management relations, have recently been expanded to include such new areas of interest as manpower and poverty problems. At the University of Toronto a new Centre for Industrial Relations has been established, a research-oriented institution whose primary objective is to further scholarly investigations into all phases of industrial relations. To launch the new Centre a conference was held with distinguished Canadian and international authorities invited to discuss the challenges and responses for Industrial Relations in the next decade, from various points of view. This volume, based on the papers presented, will be a welcome contribution to knowledge in this challenging field.

It begins with the key-note address by David A. Morse, Director-General of the International Labour Office in Geneva, who considers the general theme in terms of its world-wide ramifications, and refers to the contributions which can be made by independent research centres. The second part, entitled "Collective Bargaining in an Age of Change," contains discussions on the impact of industrial change upon our collective bargaining institutions and practices. The third part, "On the Frontier of Industrial Relations," considers two major problems: the dehumanizing aspects of industrialization and poverty.

These provocative contributions should be received with great interest by representatives of labour, management, and government, as well as by those members of the public who are concerned with the problems of a growing industrial society.

JOHN H. G. CRISPO, a graduate of the University of Toronto and the Massachusetts Institute of Technology, has taught at Huron College, University of Western Ontario and in the School of Business of the University of Toronto. He is now Director of the Centre for Industrial Relations at the University of Toronto.

INDUSTRIAL RELATIONS

CHALLENGES AND RESPONSES

The Founding Conference of the Centre for Industrial Relations, University of Toronto

edited by JOHN H. G. CRISPO

UNIVERSITY OF TORONTO PRESS

Contents

Introduction

THE FOCUS of the study of industrial relations was originally almost entirely on union-management relations as such. More recently it has expanded to include manpower and poverty problems, to name only two relatively new areas of interest. Because of the nature of its subject matter, an interdisciplinary approach has normally been taken in the study of industrial relations. This approach has contributed and doubtless will continue to contribute to our knowledge and understanding in this increasingly challenging field.

In keeping with the best traditions established by Industrial Relations Centres on other North American campuses, our new Centre will be research-oriented. Its primary objective will be to further scholarly investigations into all phases of industrial relations by both faculty members and students. But this will not preclude us from sponsoring seminars and conferences for those within the industrial relations community at large. Indeed, we look upon such activities as the best way in which to stimulate a two-way flow of communication between those studying in this field and those practising in it.

For the formal launching of our new Centre we planned a conference which would cover the full range of economic and social problems which the study of industrial relations now embraces. We chose as our theme, "Industrial Relations in the Next Decade: Challenges and Responses," and invited a number of distinguished international and Canadian authorities to address themselves to this theme from various points of view. The collection of essays which follows is the result of their efforts. Although the central theme remains intact, we have rearranged the order in which the papers were presented for publication purposes.

Part I is entitled "An International Perspective" and is devoted to the keynote address which was delivered by Mr. David A. Morse, the Director-General of the International Labour Office in Geneva, Switzerland. Mr. Morse addresses himself to the Conference's general theme in terms of its world-wide ramifications. Underlining the growing magnitude of the challenges in industrial relations which confront us all, he calls for more studied and planned responses. Only in this way, he warns, will society be able to "redress the unbalance between technological progress and social adaptation." To forestall more government involvement in this process than is absolutely essential, he urges our leading labour and management institutions to reconsider both their structural forms and their general approaches.

Part II deals with "Collective Bargaining in an Age of Change." For the most part it is devoted to a discussion of the impact of industrial change upon our collective-bargaining institutions and practices. To begin, however, we have Professor Bright's paper as a refreshing reminder that there are two schools of thought about the effect of automation upon such variables as skill and wage differentials. After breaking automation down into its various component parts, he analyses the impact of different stages of mechanization upon skill in selected manufacturing industries, and concludes that, as far as operational requirements are concerned, the more advanced the technology the more it tends to downgrade rather than upgrade the human being in the production process. He then interprets this conclusion in terms of its possible impact upon wage determination. Finally, he reviews some recent collective-bargaining innovations in this area, a review which prompts him to predict the emergence of "a salaried industrial society."

Professors Harbison and Weber assess the recent record

of collective bargaining. In a paper entitled "Collective Bargaining in Perspective," Professor Harbison engages in a wide-ranging analysis of the performance of the American collective-bargaining system to date. Although it is essentially a power relationship, he points out that collective bargaining "is a way of organizing divergent interests in such a way as to resolve rather than to extend open conflict." After stressing the limitations which are inherent in our collective-bargaining system, Professor Harbison gives it a better than passing grade on the basis of the various criteria which he spells out as being appropriate.

Essentially the same evaluation emerges from Professor Weber's treatment of "Collective Bargaining and the Challenge of Technological Change." Describing the new technology as "the second major [industrial relations] challenge of this century," he emphasizes that it "focuses on the ability of the parties to cope with dramatic alterations in the environment within which they interact." Professor Weber describes the effect which technological change is having upon the respective power of union and management, upon negotiating procedures, and upon the substantive results of collective bargaining. Like Professor Harbison, but in a narrower context, he concludes that the collective-bargaining process is continuing to make a viable contribution despite the fact that it has had to come to grips with problems it was never intended to resolve.

Professor Arthurs' presentation dovetails with those of Professors Harbison and Weber. Dealing with "Challenge and Response in the Law of Labour Relations," he explores the role of law in coping with change, especially but not exclusively of the technological variety. After voicing concern about the "cultural lag between legal and social values," he comments on the danger of the dynamics of industrial relations outstripping the ability of the legal framework to keep pace with them. He emphasizes that the "challenge for men of laws is to avoid the collision of irresistible social forces and immovable legal objects." In the industrial relations field, he suggests that this can only be done if we establish "a sort of industrial parliament" which would subject to continuous scrutiny our labour-management legislation and institutions with a view to making recommendations on how we could improve them.

The final part in this collection of essays is entitled "On the Frontier of Industrial Relations." It considers two of the many new industrial relations problems which beset us. The first of these is dealt with in a paper by Dr. Moore on "The Individual in an Organizational Society." In an attempt to escape the dehumanizing aspects of industrialization, Dr. Moore points out that man has paradoxically developed a "plethora of organizations." In our effort to contend with the fact that we are "simultaneously more specialized and differentiated" we have become "both disorganized and highly organized." If we are to contend with the real problems of the day and avoid "the perils of pluralism," Dr. Moore feels that we have only one choice. We must rethink the roles of our many institutional responses to the challenges posed by industrialization.

The final two essays deal with the newest economic and social problem to capture the public's imagination and attention. This, of course, is the matter of poverty. In an essay on "Government and Poverty," the Honourable Mr. Sauvé, Canada's Minister of Forestry and thus the minister in charge of our Agriculture Rehabilitation and Development Act, explains why governments have begun to respond in earnest to the poverty challenge. While industrialization has made many more affluent, it has by-passed numerous others and left them in dire need. At the same time it yields the wherewithal necessary to tackle the problem. After describing the tragic conditions which afflict the poverty-stricken rural family in Canada, Mr. Sauvé observes: "If, in our humane and relatively well-ordered society, such conditions can exist, I take it as an ominous indication that we have lagged dangerously in our ability to evaluate and assess the implications of the technological powers now in our possession." He then goes on to observe that while Canada is developing the resolve to attack the roots of the poverty problem, it still lacks the "community development" machinery so necessary to get on with the job.

This sets the stage for Mr. Cosgrove's paper on the American "War on Poverty." After reviewing the dimensions of the challenge posed by poverty in the U.S. and outlining the federal legislative response to date, Mr. Cosgrove turns to the social apparatus that has been set in motion to implement the new programs. The Community Action Program, rather than such agencies as the Neighborhood Youth Corps or Volunteers in Service to America, is intended to be at the heart of the American war on poverty. It is through this program that the poor themselves are directly involved in the fight to improve their way of life. As in any aspect of industrial relations the active participation of those affected is a prerequisite to an effective response to the challenge in question.

Attended by over four hundred and fifty senior labour, management, and government representatives, our Founding Conference proved an inspiration to those most active in our new Centre. It not only demonstrated public interest in and support for our undertaking but afforded us the opportunity to bring together an exceptionally strong array of informed speakers. Their presentations were so well received that we felt they deserved a wider audience. Our thanks are extended to the University of Toronto Press, in particular Miss Diane Dilworth, for assistance in making this possible.

J. H. G. C.

PART I

AN INTERNATIONAL PERSPECTIVE

1

Industrial Relations in the Next Decade

IT IS EVIDENT THAT the complex problems facing western industrialized nations are increased because of our inadequate analysis and lack of planning to meet predictable developments. While great skill and foresight is applied in the field of technical development, a widely expressed concern for the human equation is not yet matched by a similar effort. Perhaps we are really facing an economy in which, as predicted, there will be virtually no one working in the factories; the machines will regulate and repair themselves, and also determine the quantity of production. Or perhaps we can suppose that this expectation is a gross overstatement and that it will be only partially realized within relatively limited areas of industry. However, whatever the pace of development, we must all agree, before attitudes harden beyond repair and contentiousness rejects the call of reason, that our function as objective observers is to provide realistic approximations of the future, derived, not from speculation or surmise, but rather from comprehensive studies in depth. If sound industrial relations depend upon the resolution of differences, then certainly the anticipation of foreseeable problems is preferable to the sudden confrontation of change for which adequate preparation has not been made.

*Director-General, International Labour Office, Geneva, Switzerland.

It is too much to expect that the active participants engaged in the process of resolving industrial conflict can shed their ingrained attitudes and necessarily partisan interests to view the problem as objectively as it merits. It remains rather for industrial relations centres and similar bodies, which meet the standards of objectivity and competence, to analyse and to project the consequences of change in the industrial scene, and to produce benchmarks which the decision-makers may adopt, reject, or modify.

The advanced countries of Western Europe and North America are obviously on the threshold of burgeoning industrial application of technical changes which are rapidly moving beyond the planning stage. The impact on workers and industrial relations is already becoming evident. But the extent to which both labour organizations and management will be equipped to meet the challenge may in some measure depend on the degree of preparation provided in a calm, reflective atmosphere rather than in the heated crucible of conflict between hostile and suspicious attitudes.

Some obvious questions are suggested: are current collective-bargaining practices sufficiently flexible? Will changes in union structure and government policies result? Will the collective agreement as presently conceived require drastic alteration? Are we to anticipate radical variations in the familiar techniques and procedures of contemporary industrial relations? These are recurring questions which must be faced and are likely to be answered within the next decade. The task for the western countries will be to redress the imbalance between technological progress and social adaptation; to develop social institutions and structures which are appropriate to this new age; and, above all, to provide men and women with the education which will enable them to participate intelligently and responsibly in the life of a modern society.

The events of the last months and weeks have made it clear that the world is passing through one of those dangerous moments of global change in international affairs into which history seems to plunge us every twenty or so years. The ideological differences which characterize the East-West relationship are today being aggravated by a world which is divided into rich and poor nations. This division is motivated more by economics than by doctrine. The people of the developing regions no longer accept as inevitable their secular condition of poverty; and the prevailing economic and social structures in those regions will become less and less acceptable to them. The crucial question is whether these structures will be swept aside in a wave of violent revolutionary change, which would have immeasurable consequences for the peace of the world, or whether they can be peacefully adapted to the aspirations of the poverty-stricken nations. Whatever short-term political solutions may be found to alleviate the tensions in the less developed regions, I believe that the only long-term solution is to eliminate the causes of conflict by narrowing the economic gap, by raising the standards of living and, above all, by promoting conditions favouring peaceful social evolution.

In the cataclysm of change which churns on in the world, one of the most important elements of stability has been, and will continue to be, the continued prosperity and economic growth of the Western industrialized countries. This prosperity is now regarded by the less developed countries as the starting point to their international policies. A sudden and rapid decline in the economic activity of the industrialized countries would at best seriously impair their ability to assist developing countries, and at worst produce a state of international economic chaos which could lead to conflict. For a number of reasons, which go beyond purely domestic needs, emphasis is going to be placed on increased economic growth in the industrialized nations. This policy has serious implications for industrial relations, since outmoded systems and practices serve to slow down the process of growth. We must find ways to release all our prospects for growth. Thus, we find industrial relations at the very centre of our economic fabric, both for ourselves, nationally, and for the world we live in. I feel it necessary to point to this world-wide consideration, because it emphasizes the importance of the subject which concerns us, and to me it presents very strong additional reasons to believe that we will need to approach the issues which will have to be faced in the coming years with an entirely new state of mind.

I should like to review these issues under two broad headings: firstly, the drive for efficiency, which will increasingly dominate the economic policies of countries in the industrialized world, and, secondly, the growing tendency of industrial nations in the West to shape their economic and social future by means of deliberate public policy.

The drive for efficiency will be very largely characterized by the growing spread of advanced technology in industry, which we refer to as "automation." This is an indispensable condition for faster growth; and because it is of such vital importance, it will be necessary to ensure that the potential benefits of automation to society as a whole will not be lost through inefficient and uneconomic practices in industry. The issues to which automation gives rise on the industrial relations scene vary between North America and Western Europe. North America continues to suffer from unemployment for which automation is often held responsible; while in some Western European countries unemployment has almost entirely disappeared in spite of the rapid pace of automation and modernization. The main problem there is to combine full employment with increased productivity and price stability. But in both areas increasing doubts are being expressed as to the ability of traditional collective-bargaining practices to cope with the issues involved in a way that is consistent both with the principles of social justice and with the requirements of economic growth.

Basically, collective bargaining is at a crossroads because automation itself has given rise to nation-wide problems of adjustment which cannot be dealt with at the bargaining table at the plant or industry level, and need to be dealt with on a nation-wide basis. Among such problems are measures for the development of depressed areas, for the redistribution of income, for the promotion of labour mobility to ensure the rational distribution of manpower, for overhauling the educational and training systems, and so on.

Some theoreticians will reply that collective bargaining was never intended to deal with such problems. This is, of course, true; but it does not alter the fact that in countries committed to policies of full employment and rapid growth—which all countries of Western Europe and North America are—measures such as these need to be taken today at the national level. It does not alter the fact that the solution to many of the present economic and social problems of a country has passed beyond the scope of collective bargaining as it is presently conceived and practised. And it ignores the fact that there are trade unions which through their strength and representative character have been accepted as a fundamentally important element in the country, associated with government in dealing with economic, social, and fiscal issues which go beyond the traditionally accepted trade union functions and which vest the trade union movement with a responsibility not merely to its membership but to the community as a whole.

The need for a new look at collective bargaining goes even. further. Its adequacy as an instrument even for dealing with the issues for which it has traditionally been responsible—the fixing of wages and conditions of employment—is being called into question. These issues arise particularly in Western Europe where the almost general attainment of full employment has completely changed the conditions in which collective bargaining takes place. In some countries, and in some industries, unions have acquired almost unlimited power to push up their members' incomes, and employers, whose bargaining powers have correspondingly declined, tend, in conditions of labour scarcity, to bid up wages and hoard labour in order to maintain a labour force superfluous to their present requirements. Such practices are putting a severe strain on national economies and, by creating strong inflationary pressures, seriously threaten the maintenance of normal growth rates and the social objective that economic growth seeks to achieve.

This is why I foresee, as the second major challenge to industrial relations in the next decade, an increasing tendency for governments to intervene in order to restore the balance in collective bargaining. In Europe this tendency has perhaps proceeded further than in North America in the sense that institutions have been set up to enable the government to influence the outcome of collective wage bargaining and price increases and to shape the economic and social future of the country. But even in the United States, where similar institutions do not exist, the executive branch has been playing an influential role in major collective-bargaining issues.

I am not, of course, suggesting that we shall, in the near future, see the disappearance of collective bargaining from the industrial scene. Nor do I envisage an economy directed and controlled by bureaucrats. What I do foresee is a new dimension being added to collective bargaining and new functions being undertaken by labour and management. For if labour and management wish to avoid the increasing interference of public authorities on the industrial scene, then they will have to be prepared to advance and meet their responsibilities, particularly in the formation of policy at the national level, and to prove beyond doubt that voluntary action on the part of labour and management in the industrial scene has produced, and will continue to produce, better and more generally acceptable results than could be obtained by central administrative intervention. Such tripartite consultations have been growing in importance and in frequency in recent years and will doubtless continue to do so. Whether or not they will be institutionalized in national economic councils as they are in France, the United Kingdom, and Canada, or will remain relatively informal as in the President's Labour Management Advisory Committee in the United States, will vary from country to country. The important aspect of this trend is that it will enable the procedures and substantive results of industrial relations systems to be judged more critically in relation to their compatibility with the public interest, and that labour and management will be associated in the definition of what the public interest is.

The big question of the next decade is not so much whether governments will continue to take an active part in the shaping of the economy and of society—that is, I believe, beyond doubt —as whether management and trade unions will be prepared to extend their active and constructive collaboration to government in this task and will be able to commit their members to a mutually determined policy. This question is causing, and will continue to cause, much soul-searching and serious rethinking among trade unions and management. The final issue is by no means a foregone conclusion.

In most countries there has been very little clear progress towards negotiation and significant mutual commitments on such issues as income policies and productivity. One major reason is that neither the trade union movement nor, in most cases, the employers are organized in ways enabling effective agreements to be negotiated for industry or for the economy as a whole. In some countries, the centre of organizational gravity is at the level of the individual industry. In others, it is at the plant level. But in very few countries is it at the top. Thus, the challenge is, to a large extent, a challenge to the traditional structure of labour and industry, and attempts to change this structure have so far borne few concrete results.

In Europe the same problem will be found at the international level; for the introduction of "medium-term programming" at the level of the European Economic Community will bring to the fore the question of employer and worker participation in community-wide decision-making, and the restructuring of their national organizations to make such participation possible.

Whether trade unions and employers' organizations, during the next ten years, will be able to respond constructively to this challenge, I hesitate to predict. Reactions will vary considerably from country to country; and much will doubtless depend on the economic awareness of the union members and whether or not there is a genuine willingness to play a major policy role in society as a whole. However, the challenges to industrial relations cannot only, or even primarily, be considered as challenges to structure. They are also challenges to the functions and the social purpose of the parties in the industrial relations system.

This is particularly true of trade unions. Trade unions will, in the coming years, have to undergo a complete reappraisal of their role in society. In a sense they have become victims of their own success. There can be no doubt that if living and working conditions have improved so radically in the past few decades, if the great majority of workers today enjoy a standard of living which would have been quite inconceivable twenty or thirty years ago, this is very largely due to the energetic struggles waged by trade unions on behalf of their members. But it is precisely because they have fought so hard, and with such success, for the rights and status of the working man, that unions need to widen their functions and role in society. They have achieved a strong bargaining position and they are using it to increase the share of affluence for their members. But they are no longer defending working people from starvation. Their members are no longer the underdogs of society. The under- dogs are the unemployed, the poor, the aged, the oppressed, the underprivileged, who continue to exist in our so-called affluent societies, but whose interests the trade unions in most countries today are not equipped to defend as energetically as they could or should like to, in spite of their long and honour- able tradition as spokesmen for the less fortunate.

A further problem confronting most of the traditional trade union movements of the Western world is the fact that techno- logical change is eroding the basis of their membership; the number of manual blue-collar workers, who constitute the backbone of the trade union movement, is declining steadily each year, and will probably continue to decline as the years go by. And most trade union movements are not being particu- larly successful in attracting into their ranks the growing army of non-manual clerical and professional workers. It is possible that the growing strength of professional workers will give rise to the emergence of new types of unions, some of which may be outside the traditional union movement, performing func- tions which are akin to collective bargaining. Professional associations of doctors, nurses, teachers, and government employees may, in the future, increasingly assume union-like functions and become part of the industrial relations scene, bargaining for the regulation of incomes and conditions of work.

Another aspect of change is likely to be greater concentra- tion of authority and control in the parent unions. As I have said, industry rather than plant bargaining may become a more effective vehicle for resolving major problems, such as that of labour mobility. Unions will find increasing need for professional aids to meet the industrial engineering utilized by management. Greater involvement by the unions in the training and retraining of displaced workers will underscore the need for specialists in establishing and operating training programs. At the collective-bargaining table the effects of increased automation will impose on the union bargainers responsibility for matching the technical knowledge of their management counterparts.

The question that all this suggests is whether the traditional union movement is going to become a less significant and constantly declining force in society, or can emerge, reinforced and reinvigorated, to fulfil new and responsible functions. Further, what new functions can unions reasonably be expected to undertake without compromising their independence and without losing the support of their members?

I think it is quite conceivable that the unions may take on, to a greater extent than hitherto, a number of activities beneficial to the entire community rather than just to their own membership. It is, of course, true that unions in virtually all countries already make their voices heard on a wide range of national issues which are not immediately connected with their functions as bargainers on behalf of their members. In the United States, for example, they have taken a definite stand in favour of civil rights, the war against poverty, and other important issues. However, the community may expect them in the years to come to take more initiatives themselves and to be more active and constructive in their criticism or support of government initiatives. This may in some countries, as I have suggested earlier, involve them in actual participation in the formulation of national policies. But even if unions are unwilling or unable to take that big and decisive step, it will be possible for them to play a constructive part in society outside formal machinery for participation.

Moreover, there might be a change of emphasis in their action as bargainers at the plant and industry level. There may be a greater effort by union negotiators to adjust their action in favour of their members to the needs of the community as a whole. For example, a rapidly changing economy needs a high degree of labour mobility and governments have set up machinery to facilitate this mobility. However, the emphasis of union action appears to be on the protection of the worker's job at all costs, and this is, in some countries, impeding the rational distribution of manpower and acting as a brake on economic growth. Public opinion will in future expect trade unions and their members to view redundancy as an opportunity for improvement rather than as a cause of distress. Trade unions will be asked more and more to serve their members by helping to facilitate movement to new jobs, new occupations, or new regions rather than by placing emphasis on the maintenance of the *status quo*. It remains to be seen whether unions will be prepared to change their policies so radically and, if so, subject to what conditions?

If unions are able to develop the more positive aspect of their role not only as agents for social improvement, but also as agents for economic growth and efficiency, we may see emerging a far greater community of interest between management and labour and possibilities might open up for a much greater degree of mutual confidence and co-operation between them than has characterized their relations in the past. As an example of an area where such co-operation is of vital importance, I should like to refer to my 1957 Report on *Automation and Other Technological Developments* to the International Labour Conference, where I stated that the primary demands of unions in a variety of industrial countries is for joint consultation at an early stage of development, continuing through installation and operation of the new technology. Such consultation can be materially enlarged at the instance of students of the problem who are not directly involved with the competing position unfortunately characteristic of industrial relations. Since automation by its very nature is not a sudden phenomenon but requires comprehensive advanced planning, adequate opportunity exists to study and prepare in advance for many of the labour problems which can be anticipated. I foresee an increasing awareness in the next decade of the need for such joint planning stimulated in some measure by factual studies and reasoned conclusions.

I know that in Canada and the United States new bases for labour-management co-operation are being sought. And in several industrialized countries in Western Europe experiments have been made with new forms of "industrial democracy" which would extend this co-operation to joint decision-making in the plant. I should not be surprised to see further developments in this direction in a number of other countries. This, however, raises a whole range of questions. Are unions gradually going to lose their position as bargainers to become co-operators or partners in management as well as in government? Will it be possible for them to combine the two functions? If their bargaining function becomes more limited, will this not lose them the support of their more militant members? Will there be a split in union movement and the emergence of two types of unionism—the militant, bargaining union on the one hand, and, on the other, the union actively participating in the formation of policy at the plant, industry, and national levels?

It would be rash, I think, to try to give a definite and absolute answer to these questions, which have very serious and far-reaching implications for the trade union movement and society as a whole. Only experience will show whether trade unions are able to fulfil new functions and, at the same time, maintain their position as militant champions of their members' rights. To maintain this position, certain new demands can already be foreseen. Without doubt unions will emphasize increasingly the extension of seniority on a much broader base. Emphasis may also be anticipated for the liberalizing and extension of dismissal and severance pay provisions, coupled with reductions in service requirements for eligibility and increase in the benefits. Demands for an increase of paid holidays and paid vacations will also recur, as will demands for guaranteed wage and unemployment plans, as a means of reducing the impact of technological displacement. Perhaps the most pressing issue is to be in the area of improved pensions. Here the bargainers must resolve the claims for vesting and portability of benefits. With this will undoubtedly come pressure for more favourable earlier retirement and the funding of plans.

One thing is clear. Union officials and union negotiators will even more than today have to become "broader gauged," with a clear awareness of the needs of the nation as well as of their own members, and also seek to educate their members at the shop level to that awareness.

This will, I think, have a direct bearing on the future of the union's basic weapon—the strike. It is increasingly being stressed that strikes are a very costly way of settling disputes. Industrial machinery is today so staggeringly expensive and the industrial processes have become so interdependent that a single, limited strike can seriously affect the growth of the nation's economy. There is therefore likely to be much greater concern with the need to eliminate the causes of strikes; and this will place a heavy burden of responsibility on management. For strikes can very often be traced back to poor relations and a poor working atmosphere in the plant.

The challenge of the next decade will therefore be as great for management as for unions. Public irritation is being increasingly expressed in some countries at management's failure often to eliminate inefficient and restrictive practices and generally to provide the necessary leadership in the plant. Until recently, it was possible to say that this was management's concern and no one else's. If a manager could not manage his plant according to the basic rules of efficiency, then he had to suffer the consequences. However, today it is the community as a whole which has to suffer the consequences in the form of increased prices, inflationary spirals, and an adverse balance of payments. In the future, society will more and more expect unions and their members to exercise restraint and at the same time expect management to bear its share of the responsibility for maintaining an efficient national economy.

The challenge to management in the years ahead will therefore be to combine efficient production with good relations in the plant. And management will need to be as aware of its responsibilities to its workers as it is to its shareholders. The industrial undertaking will be viewed to a far greater extent by managers and workers alike as a social unit in whose proper functioning both sides and the community at large have a common interest Perhaps the growing gulf separating industrial ownership from management may make this objective easier to achieve, for it is already creating, as we all know, a new and differently oriented managerial class. Management will, in the years to come, increasingly become a highly professionalized job, based on highly professionalized training combining technical qualifications with a sense of leadership. Managers will have to be able to co-ordinate skilfully the technical and the human aspects of industrial management; they will have to be the bridge builders between the technicians, scientists, and efficiency experts on the one hand and the workers on the other.

Thus, I anticipate quite significant changes in the organization and practices of an industrial plant. I expect that the still rather sharp distinction between the technical and clerical staff and the manual workers will gradually disappear. I expect further experiments to be made in industrial democracy which might in some cases extend to the sharing of decision-making between management and workers, but which will at least comprise regular and frequent consultation on matters of common interest as is the case in Sweden today. Perhaps a more conscious consideration of these problems in the day-to-day administration of companies may offer an opportunity for management to take the views of their employees more fully into account. It will be argued that these and similar innovations will contribute greatly to avoiding the misunderstandings, mismanagement, and neglect of the workers' needs and aspirations which have in the past led to considerable industrial unrest, to inefficiency, and generally, to a slowing down of the growth of the whole economy.

I have laid great emphasis in this statement on the need for responsible management and responsible trade union leadership. This requires education in the widest sense of the word. In the context of industrial relations it requires education which will equip the leaders of industry and of trade unions to exercise their functions competently and with a high sense of responsibility towards the society to which they belong. I would thus add that if Western countries want to modernize their system of industrial relations, they will need to begin by taking a new look at the ways in which the leaders of tomorrow's industrial societies are trained, prepared, recruited, and educated for positions of responsibility.

I should like to make just one more reflection on the society in which we shall live in the next decade. It is important, as I have attempted to stress at various points, that the overriding concern of nations in the Western industrialized world should be to put their economies in top gear and to eliminate as far as possible all institutions and practices which can slow down the process of growth. In particular, they will need to avoid conflict wherever it can be avoided since conflict in a modern, booming society is too costly to support. We shall, in other words, be living in societies dominated by the desire to seek a consensus, and constantly evolving and experimenting with new ways to democratize and make more effective the process of consensus-seeking.

This preoccupation with consensus-seeking must not, however, mean placing further restrictions on the fundamental human freedoms to which Western nations have traditionally been so attached. A consensus which actually reflects the interests and aspirations of all the forces in society is not a negation of freedom; on the contrary, it can only serve to strengthen the social and economic fabric of a free society. What we need to aim at is not a society in which limitations are placed on freedom of expression and freedom of action, but rather an educated society of responsible men and women capable of looking beyond their own immediate interests to those of the community and, indeed, those of the world at large; leaders concerned with developing the individual personality and community as a whole. To achieve such a society will call for courage, imagination, new thinking, ability, and ingenuity from the leadership of both sides of industry. The challenge therefore to leaders of industry and labour in the years which lie ahead will be to their statesmanship and to their vision—both important elements in the development of the democratic world. I believe that in the next decade Western society will move in this direction and in doing so will make a significant contribution to the removal of the ideological and economic barriers which at present divide mankind and threaten the peace and stability of the world.

PART II

COLLECTIVE BARGAINING IN AN AGE OF CHANGE

2

Automation and Wage Determination

JAMES R. BRIGHT*

DURING THE 1950's a wave of mechanization, directed toward more automatic manufacturing systems, swept throughout American industry. Although automatic manufacturing systems were not new in concept or fact,[1] the breadth of industrial effort, the degree of advances sought, the functions mechanized, and public and union response to these mechanization programs evoked national interest unparalleled in American

*Professor, Harvard University, Graduate School of Business Administration. This paper is based on the author's early publications in the United States and Germany, which are consolidated and updated for a Canadian audience.

[1]Highly automatic manufacturing systems were conceived, designed, and operated as such, over roughly the past 200 years. For example: Oliver Evans built an automatic grist mill in Delaware in 1794; and in 1802–8, Marc Brunel developed in England a highly mechanized system for manufacturing ship's pulley blocks that was in use until 1854. During the early 1800's a mechanized system for making hard tack (ship's biscuits) was installed at the Deptford (England) naval stores post. In the 1880's the Waltham Watch Company (Massachusetts) developed a transfer machine for automatic watch-making. During 1913–15, mechanized moving assembly lines were developed at Ford Motor Company in Detroit. In 1919–20 the A. O. Smith Corporation (Milwaukee) built an automatic frame assembly line which, in the words of their President, was "a plant to run without men." It used 200 men and produced 420 automobile frames per hour. With the exception of the electric lamp industry, it was probably the most noteworthy effort at automatic manufacturing of discrete parts until recent times. The textile industry of the 1800's and the oil industry of the 1920's actually were "automated" to a greater degree than are many other industries today. However, familiarity has dimmed their significance as feats of highly automatic processing.

industrial history. The definitions of automation were numerous and varied; opinions on its impact were the same, and continue to be so to this day.

Out of the furor the major issues that gradually emerged revolved around people and jobs. That labour needed special forms of protection against the power of automation to displace (or replace) workers, and that automation altered the educational needs of the work force so extremely as to require higher education, special training, or substantial retraining efforts were especially timely issues because rising labour costs, booming postwar demand, and new technical possibilities encouraged many managements and engineers to build highly automatic and extensively integrated production systems. As "automation" dramatized the threat of displacement to labour, it also symbolized a goal to management.

The effects of automation on jobs are the very heart of proper wage determination, and of social readjustments, education, and retraining problems. Therefore, I ask the reader to follow this attempt at a critical analysis of the effects of increasing mechanization in industrial jobs. Against this background we can then consider, more rationally, the appropriateness of various wage determination automation developments.

TRENDS IN THE MECHANIZATION OF WORK

By analysing the function of new machinery (including highly automatic systems) in manufacturing, distribution, and the office, we can see that, whether or not the term "automation"[2] is applied, we are dealing with the mechanization of all physical and some mental activities including:

[2]In this paper I shall use the term "automation" in the way it is widely used in society; as a very loose synonym for "more highly automatic" and as a succinct way of expressing technological progress built largely upon mechanization. Each increment of mechanization simply is the automatic (non-human) performance of a bit of an activity. The notion that automation is due to a special kind of mechanization, or special kind of automatic action, based upon feedback control, is a naive error. The term did not originate around feedback control; it originated around automatic movement. Furthermore, systematic analysis of automatic machinery and of so called "automated" production systems demonstrates repeatedly that

1. Direct labour tasks, with growing emphasis on assembly work;

2. Materials handling; including movement between machines, departments, building, carrier loading, and machine loading (work feeding);

3. Testing and inspection; including the check-out of complex systems;

4. Distribution functions including packaging, storage, order picking, transportation, and discharge to point of use;

5. Communications functions, including the collection, transmission, recording, storage, generation and duplication of verbal, visual, and written information (e.g., two-way radio, air tubes, industrial TV, tape recorders, tape-controlled typewriters). We also see the spread of the computer and related equipment, associated with items above, to mechanize all or part of many intellectual processes;

6. Data processing, including the acquisition, selection, manipulation, comparison, recall, and display of words and numbers;

7. Design and analysis activities, in which the machinery constructs a set of procedures or manipulates data appropriate to a desired complex relationship;

8. Control, in which physical conditions or natural characteristics are sensed, comparisons made and appropriate action taken by combinations of the above equipment. This includes both feedback and program control devices.

The intensity of this mechanization, its widespread applications, and the highly automatic nature of the new machinery systems suggest some disturbing problems. These apply not only to the blue-collar worker, but also to the white-collar worker and even to some management functions. I shall leave

relatively little feedback control is found in these automatic machinery systems. Also, a step-by-step review of systems employing some feedback control will show that those systems are not automatic solely because of the control but also because of the integrated mechanization of all necessary activities. For specific analyses of "automated" systems see the "mechanization profiles" in my research study, *Automation and Management* (Boston: Division of Research, Graduate School of Business Administration, Harvard University, 1958).

the question of the displacement caused by automation for those who have more valid and useful statistics than I have been able to find. Our question will be: How does automatic machinery change the demand on the worker?

In simple terms the popular and apparently logical reasoning runs like this: Automation results in machinery of a more automatic nature directed by highly automatic controls. The employees manning and servicing this equipment need a higher degree of understanding, alertness, and education. They will require additional training, higher types of skills, and even new levels of education. Thus, the job content of individual tasks associated with the new machinery will require more skill. "Upgrading" is obvious. Moving beyond the individual and looking at the factory as a whole, it becomes clear that the factory payroll will have to include more skilled and fewer unskilled persons. Furthermore, automatic machinery will eliminate many low-skill workers and put relatively highly skilled operators in their places. Meanwhile, the maintenance force will have to be expanded, proportionally. A more highly skilled work force is, therefore, inevitable and essential. The same reasoning applies to white-collar workers associated with mechanization of business systems, especially those associated with the computer.

This common train of thought, so logical and persuasive, leads to two general points of view. Many managers, machinery manufacturers, engineers, and automation enthusiasts have held that upgrading is the blessing of automation. It will relieve labour of drudgery and of dirty, unsafe, or monotonous work. The superior levels of education and training required deserve, and will command, higher prestige and pay for the worker.

The other point of view so vehemently expressed by many labour leaders, but also supported by some social scientists, popular writers, and politicians, originates from the same premises and concludes, "Exactly so!" Spokesmen then proceed to a logical and alarming end. Not only will the average worker be displaced by the higher productivity of the automatic equipment; he will be barred from the plant because he lacks the education, training, and skill necessary to hold one of the automated jobs. The automated plant thus becomes a technological lock-out for the common man. Elaborate retraining programs, and legislation to soften the blow to affected labour are therefore an urgent social necessity. The displacement costs caused by automation are a price that should not be paid by the displaced worker, and the logical underwriters of social readjustment are the firms using automatic equipment and/or the government. Furthermore, it is obvious that the upgraded worker on automated systems deserves more money for his superior skill and "responsibility."

Are these sweeping generalizations about "upgrading" effects of automation on firm ground? I hold that they are not. We stand to make some serious mistakes in legislation, in industrial planning, in social planning, and in wage policies because of failure to appreciate that mechanization can have a variety of effects on the individual job depending upon the specific character of the new equipment, the degree of change between the old and the new job, and the shift in duties assigned to the individual as a result of these changes.

In this paper, I shall concentrate on the *operating* work force in highly mechanized (automated) plants; and first will consider the idea that wages must or should be increased to reflect the increased "skill" required of the worker.

It is not my purpose to argue that increased worker contribution should not be rewarded. I firmly believe that greater contributions deserve greater rewards in all of society. I only propose to demonstrate that this common train of reasoning is based on the fallacious assumption that more demands are placed on the worker with every advance in automation. This does not always, or even often, happen. Hence, all the arguments, agreements, plans, and procedures to base wage determinations around "increased skill requirements" and "upgrading" lead to hopeless inconsistencies, and cannot provide a sound base for wage adjustments or social planning.

During the several years which I spent in field research on

managerial problems in so-called automated plants and in exploring automation with industrialists, government personnel, social scientists, and other researchers, I did not find that the upgrading effect had occurred to anywhere near the extent that is often assumed. On the contrary, there was more evidence that automation often had reduced the skill requirements of the operating work force, and occasionally of the entire factory force including the maintenance organization.[3] I found frequent instances in which management's stated belief that automation had required a higher calibre of work-force skill was refuted when the facts were explored. Other managers admitted, and on several occasions emphasized, that they had made substantial errors in assigning high wage rates to some automated jobs. These wage rates not only proved to be out of line with the difficulty of the task but were unfair in contrast to the wages of employees working with conventional machinery. The training time for some key jobs was reduced to a fraction of the former figure.[4] Later studies reflect many similar findings.

Why, then, has this common misunderstanding developed and persisted? I believe it is because we have not widely appreciated the following points:

Automation is not an absolute condition or quality. The so-called automated systems and plants have different degrees and amounts of mechanized performance. The "labour effect" of "automating" a job depends on precisely what functions are mechanized, and what degree or level of mechanization is employed.

"Skill" needed by the worker is a loose and inadequate expression of the demand on a worker in a task. As will be explained, the worker may need to bring up to twelve different contributions to a job. This mix of contributions is unique "before and after" automation. The net effect of automation on the worker's job, therefore, can only be determined by seeing

[3]For results of this research see the chaps. 11, 12, and 13 on maintenance and the work force in Bright, *Automation and Management*.
[4]*Ibid.*, see chap. 12.

how each of these twelve types of contribution was affected by this particular advance in automation.

The general concept of rising, then falling demand on the worker as automation progresses makes it clear why statements or predictions of a universal end effect of automation will yield erroneous conclusions much of the time. The impact on each worker is not just a result of end conditions at a given level of mechanization. The effect is the result of changing from one level of mechanization to another. Therefore, what counts most is the *net* difference in demand on the worker between his original job and his automated job.

There is a general lack of appreciation of the evolutionary nature of machinery. This process of evolution is clearly established by Usher with respect to individual machines,[5] and I have extended it to the automated line factory which is, I believe, simply the design (synthesis) of a machine on a grander scale.[6] No thoughtful student of labour mechanization problems should neglect the study of the evolution of the tools with which labour works. Usher's study reveals the directions of machine design, the process of refinement, the move toward increasing constraint and control, the simplification of mechanisms for performing given actions, and the great increase in reliability with successive generations of machines. This evolution explains, in part, why "responsibility" of the operator, as a job contribution, rapidly decreases with refinement of machinery systems.

Closely allied to the above is the general failure to appreciate the decline in the need for operator "knowledge" and "responsibility" at the higher levels of mechanization. When processes are first automated, they usually require the operator to detect, act, and maybe to correct malfunctions. Hence responsibility is very great on semi-automated jobs. But as automation advances, the machine is given the power to detect trouble, and then to correct its performance. As reliability of

[5]Albert Payson Usher, *A History of Mechanical Inventions* (rev. ed., Cambridge, Mass.: Harvard University Press, 1965), pp. 116 ff.
[6]Bright, *Automation and Management*, pp. 15–16.

these sensing-correcting mechanisms increases, and it inevitably does in later generations of machines, the operator literally loses the opportunity to exercise "responsibility" even though the machine may be more complicated and costly.

Another cause for misunderstanding is failure to discriminate between operators as such, and "operators" who have, by management choice or necessity, been given elements of set-up and maintenance duties which may demand much higher skill and training. If responsibility for secondary and tertiary support functions is given to the "operator," we undoubtedly have substantially altered the nature of the work and "skill" required. But it should be recognized that this reassignment of duties has not invalidated the effects of increasing automation on job content. Rather, we have, in such instances, deliberately enlarged the job.

Most important of all is the general lack of appreciation of the nature of machine design progress. Machine designers are directed by the basic economic laws of supply and demand; and they too are aided by new technical capabilities. In line with Usher's theory, they continually are mechanizing difficult elements of operator tasks, and are correcting unreliable machinery. They also are mechanizing the high skill, high education jobs. Note that automation includes the mechanization of trouble detection and alarm, trouble shooting, set-up, and even engineering design work. Consider that in maintenance work we see the commonplace act of automatic lubrication, the more exciting feats of automatic signalling of trouble, and the incredibly fast, accurate, and computerized check-out of aircraft and space vehicles, power plants, process industries, communications systems, and even of some computers themselves. Similarly, the difficult job of set-up is being mechanized by tape-controlled machine tools and punch card control of many processes. We can expect that machine designers will mechanize and simplify other new, difficult tasks.

Finally, there is the set of special conditions surrounding the debugging period, and the unique, first-of-its-kind automation. During these pioneering periods maintenance will be high, trouble shooting difficult and time-consuming, and the responsibility for fast and proper action will be great. The manning of automated systems at these times may very likely require exceptional contributions. Whatever wage arrangements are made for this period should not be confused with wage standards for normal conditions.

The "Skilled Worker"

Automaticity does not inevitably mean lack of opportunity for the unskilled worker. On the contrary, automated machinery tends to require less operator skill after certain levels of mechanization are achieved. It seems that the average worker often will master different jobs more quickly and easily if highly automatic machinery is used. Confirming evidence shows that many so-called key jobs, currently requiring long experience and training, are being reduced to easily learned, machine-tending jobs. To understand how this can be, let us examine the demands machinery makes on the worker.

Perhaps the best way to start is by asking: what kinds of contributions does the worker make to production tasks? We could say that in general the worker receives compensation for the following twelve things: (1) physical effort; (2) mental effort; (3) manipulative skill; (4) general skill; (5) education; (6) experience; (7) exposure to hazards; (8) undesirable job conditions; (9) responsibility; (10) decision-making; (11) influence on productivity; and (12) seniority. While these contributions might be explained in more detail, the concept seems valid: that is, there are different physical and mental activities which every worker contributes to a production task. Disagreement about these activities shows also that the phrase, "skilled worker," has a highly subjective connotation. Certainly these words are not used consistently by many of us, or uniformly by industry or labour.

It is immediately apparent that not all of these demands or contributions are equally important in a given task, nor are they of a constant relative importance from one production task to another. In even a simple activity the worker's contribution can vary depending on the equipment used. Consider, for instance, the physical effort of a construction worker using

INITIATING CONTROL SOURCE	TYPE OF MACHINE RESPONSE		POWER SOURCE	LEVEL NUMBER	LEVEL OF MECHANIZATION
FROM A VARIABLE IN THE ENVIRONMENT	RESPONDS WITH ACTION	MODIFIES OWN ACTION OVER A WIDE RANGE OF VARIATION	MECHANICAL (NONMANUAL)	17	ANTICIPATES ACTION REQUIRED AND ADJUSTS TO PROVIDE IT.
				16	CORRECTS PERFORMANCE WHILE OPERATING.
				15	CORRECTS PERFORMANCE AFTER OPERATING.
		SELECTS FROM A LIMITED RANGE OF POSSIBLE PRE-FIXED ACTIONS		14	IDENTIFIES AND SELECTS APPROPRIATE SET OF ACTIONS.
				13	SEGREGATES OR REJECTS ACCORDING TO MEASUREMENT.
				12	CHANGES SPEED, POSITION, DIRECTION ACCORDING TO MEASUREMENT SIGNAL.
	RESPONDS WITH SIGNAL			11	RECORDS PERFORMANCE.
				10	SIGNALS PRESELECTED VALUES OF MEASUREMENT (INCLUDES ERROR DETECTION).
				9	MEASURES CHARACTERISTIC OF WORK.
FROM A CONTROL MECHANISM THAT DIRECTS A PREDETERMINED PATTERN OF ACTION	FIXED WITHIN THE MACHINE			8	ACTUATED BY INTRODUCTION OF WORK PIECE OR MATERIAL.
				7	POWER TOOL SYSTEM, REMOTE CONTROLLED.
				6	POWER TOOL, PROGRAM CONTROL (SEQUENCE OF FIXED FUNCTIONS).
				5	POWER TOOL, FIXED CYCLE (SINGLE FUNCTION).
FROM MAN	VARIABLE			4	POWER TOOL, HAND CONTROL.
				3	POWERED HAND TOOL.
			MANUAL	2	HAND TOOL.
				1	HAND.

wheelbarrow and shovel *versus* the skill, mental effort, and experience required to use a bulldozer on the same job. Therefore, to understand how automation affects the work force skills we must consider how each of the demands in any given job is affected by increasing degrees of mechanization and automatic control.

Mechanization is not an equivalent thing in every production system. One production line is "more mechanized" than another. Wherein lies the difference? Part of the explanation is that mechanization has at least three fundamental qualities or dimensions: (*a*) span—the extent to which mechanization spreads across a sequence of production events; (*b*) level—the degree of mechanical accomplishment by which a given production action is performed, reflecting in part the fact that automatic control leads to increasing sophistication in the response of the machinery to environmental conditions;[7] and, (*c*) penetration—the extent to which secondary and tertiary production tasks, such as lubrication, adjustment, and repair are mechanized.

We can examine the characteristics of mechanical performance by analysing how tools refine and supplement man's abilities. This analysis can be arranged and related in a chart, as in Chart 1. A distinct evolution is apparent in these levels.

First, there is the substitution of mechanical power for manual effort, which takes some burden from the worker (after level 2). Then, as increasing degrees of fixed control yield the desired machine action, the worker does less and less guiding of the tool (levels 5–8). As the ability to measure is added to the machine, a portion of the control-decision information is

[7]*Ibid.*, Chap. 4 explains these levels in detail and gives "mechanization profiles" for eight "automated" plants.

CHART 1   LEVELS OF MECHANIZATION AND THEIR RELATIONSHIP TO POWER AND CONTROL SOURCES
NOTE: The concept of levels of mechanization (and the idea of a mechanization profile to measure mechanization through a manufacturing sequence) was first presented in James R. Bright, "How to Evaluate Automation," *HBR* July–August, 1955, p. 101. This analysis has since been refined and is presented in detail with explanations of each level in *Automation and Management* (Boston, 1958), pp. 39–56. All charts are reproduced courtesy *Harvard Business Review*.

mechanically obtained for the operator (after level 8). As the machine is given still higher degrees of automaticity, more and more of the decision-making and appropriate follow-up actions are performed mechanically. For instance, as the selection of necessary machine speeds, feeds, temperature control, and so on is mechanized, further "decision-making," "judgment," "experience," and even "alertness" demands are lifted from the worker (levels 12–14). Finally, the machine is given the power of "self-correction" to a minor, and then to a greater degree (levels 15–17), until the need to adjust the machine has been completely removed from the worker.

One need not accept this particular classification of "levels" to confirm the fundamental point that successive advances in automatic capability generally reduce operator tasks after certain levels are reached. By definition, the more automatic the machine, the less the operator of the machine has to do.

However, earlier we recognized that the worker's contribution on the job embraces more than a few items such as "skill" or "effort." The question, therefore, is: how is each of the possible work contributions we identified affected by increasing levels of mechanization? It seems clear that some job demands will decrease with increasing automaticity, but perhaps there are others that will increase. I have not made accurate quantitative measurements, but believe that it is worthwhile to examine several types of worker contributions and to theorize as to how they will be affected by increases in the level of mechanization.

Physical effort. If we were to chart the physical effort contributed by the worker against the level of mechanization as shown in Chart 2 it is clear that we would describe some kind of declining curve. That is, the physical effort exerted by the worker will be highest in the lower levels of mechanization, and it will decline abruptly once the fixed-cycle machines of level 5 are achieved. Notice that literally no physical effort is required after the completely automatic control of level 12 is reached, provided that work feeding and work removal have been mechanized.

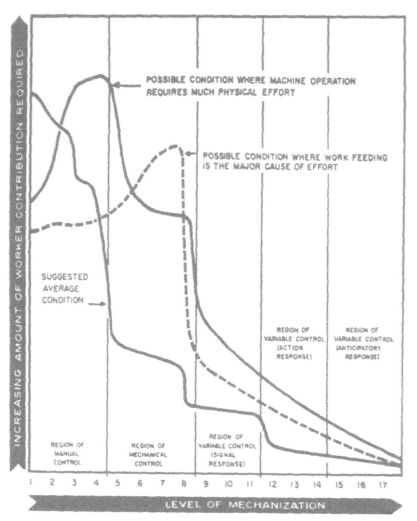

CHART 2   How Physical Effort Required of Operators May Vary
with Levels of Mechanization

Education. Is it not true that as a more complex tool is provided, the worker needs increased training in order to understand the operation of the machine, its adjustment, and its
application to a variety of tasks?

When power is applied to the tool, and adjusting regulatory devices requiring careful use to obtain proper performance are provided, the worker obviously has to learn more about the machinery—perhaps much more, if the equipment is complex. He also may need more education to understand the principles underlying the machine's operation and action on materials. Accordingly, the need for education and training definitely increases. Training a journeyman machinist takes up to four years. Apparently, though, educational need does not continue to increase as automaticity approaches still higher levels. In the metal-working field and in many other areas, the effect of automatic cycling (level 6) is to substitute workers of lesser training ("machine operators" for machinists). The reason is almost self-evident. When a pattern of predetermined actions can be mechanically achieved, there is no particular need for the understanding, the training, and the education on the part of the operator that existed when adjustment and control lay in his hands. Therefore, at some point after level 4, the education required by the worker no longer increases. For instance, after the mechanization levels introducing measurement have been reached, the critical judgment and attention required of the operator actually become less. The machine measures for him. Of course the degree and point of change will vary with equipment, but the common effect seems to be a rising-then-falling curve, as hypothesized in Chart 3. In many instances, the need for education and understanding of principles may continue well into higher levels, but these eventually become unnecessary contributions as reliability increases.

Mental effort. One of the major conclusions in the pioneer case study presented by Charles R. Walker in *Toward the Automatic Factory*[8] is a claim that mental effort is substantially increased by automacity. A number of statements in union literature and speeches also insists that the "mental effort" or

[8](New Haven: Yale University Press, 1957). See also, Charles R. Walker, "Life in the Automatic Factory," *Harvard Business Review*, Jan.–Feb., 1958, p. 111.

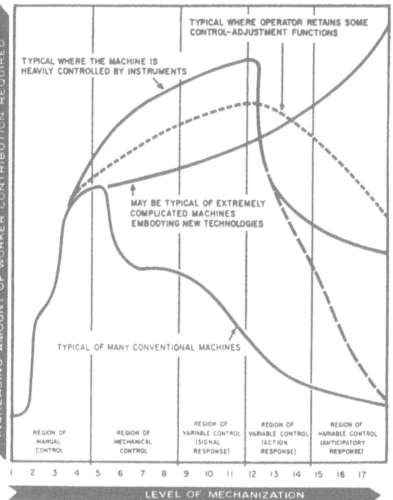

CHART 3   HOW EDUCATION REQUIRED OF OPERATORS MAY VARY WITH
LEVELS OF MECHANIZATION

strain increases with automation. Rigorous examination of our
"levels" reveals that this is not always the case.

Obviously, when he works with hand tools (levels 2 and
3) and with hand-controlled equipment (level 4), the worker

must concentrate in order to avoid misdirecting the tooling, to "control" the activity, and to detect conditions that might disrupt successful functioning. As the machine is given the power to perform by itself, the desired sequence of events (levels 5 and 6), and the need for concentration on the actual direction of the machinery is reduced. At the same time, however, it is entirely possible that alertness to malfunctioning, to the quality of the output, and so on, becomes a far more worrisome mental task, because of faster cycling. Then, on these levels, increased mental effort or strain might be a very real thing.

Consider what happens next as the machine is given the facility for measurement on levels 9–11. In a primitive way, the machine begins to detect and to report the character of some operating conditions. Therefore, depending on just what characteristics are measured and signalled, the operator no longer needs to be quite as alert. In some instances, as with safety valves, the operator may be quite at ease until the warning signal is given to him. A number of workers on highly automatic machining lines, in which automatic gauging and signalling of performance were employed, spontaneously acknowledged this effect of automaticity when I interviewed them. These men and women stated, that they found the jobs less demanding because they were able to relax more than under former conditions. Attention, concentration, and mental effort were required only at the moment faulty performance was signalled.

The mental effort requirements seem to be reduced further as still higher levels of mechanization are employed. Here the machine not only detects the need for a modification in its performance, but it begins to make such a modification without human attention. We might say that on levels 9–11 the machine calls for human help; and on levels 12–17 the machinery adjusts itself as necessary, in an increasingly sophisticated manner. The more automatic machines employ control devices that regulate their performance to achieve the desired end without human attention. It surely must follow that "mental strain" is ultimately reduced.

How, then, can it be said that mental strain will continue to grow with increasing automaticity, as Charles Walker reported? On closer examination his findings are not contradictory at all to this theory. For, as Walker's description indicates, the steel mill he studied was not a level 17, or even a level 12 operation. The span of mechanization was broken at several points. Much of the machinery operated at levels 5 and 6 and only in a few instances throughout the manufacturing sequence was level 12 reached or exceeded. Increased mental strain had resulted not because the equipment was more automatic, but because it was not automatic enough! The systems, although more integrated, faster, and bigger, still had many "control" problems and there was potential for more serious error because of increased speed and power. Even so, after the men once learned to live with the equipment, there was (I infer from the reactions he reports) considerably less mental strain.

In sum, it is reasonable that a curve such as is shown in Chart 4 may be a typical relationship of mental effort to increasing automaticity. It is especially important to consider how widely mental effort may vary depending upon the reliability of the particular system and the consequences of failure.

Other contributions. Similarly, responsibility can be thought of as increasing with the more costly and more highly integrated machinery. However, it increases only to the extent that the worker truly has responsibility. The ultimate effect of the higher levels of automation is to remove responsibility for performance from the hands of the worker. The detection of faulty operations, of overloads, malfunction, shortages, changing material or power requirements, and so on gradually becomes vested in the machine. At some point after level 11 or 12 is achieved the control mechanism has the responsibility, not the operator.

Much the same can be said about manipulative skill. Up to about level 5 the need for physical dexterity may increase, but above that point the machine takes over more and more. The

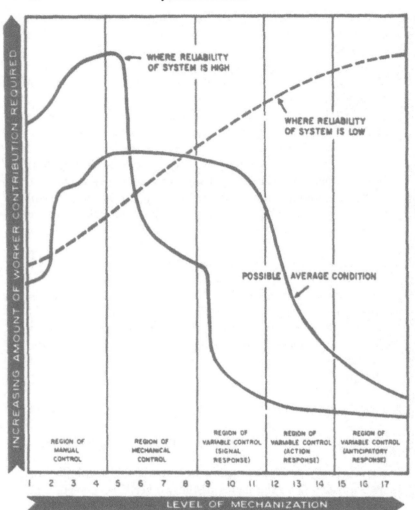

CHART 4 HOW MENTAL EFFORT REQUIRED OF OPERATORS MAY VARY
WITH LEVELS OF MECHANIZATION

need for "general" skill increases up to about level 11, but then
the machine again begins to take over and the need decreases.

One could construct similar relationships between the
demands on the worker with respect to the other contributions

mentioned earlier. While no curve could be drawn that would be universally applicable to all types of machinery, I believe that almost all such curves would exhibit the same general characteristics: that is, at some higher levels of mechanization most worker contributions would decline.

Total effect on the worker. Production jobs never require just one kind of contribution by the worker. They involve combinations of some of these contributions in different degrees. Thus it is necessary to consider some kind of combined "demand on the worker" effect. This has been done in Chart 5 which shows several curves suggesting the types of net effects on the contribution by the worker as the degree of automaticity increases. While it does not seem possible to prove quantitatively that these curves are correct, they are substantiated in concept by many observations of actual automated job requirements in industry.

It would be a mistake, of course, to assume that the reduction of job content is the only effect of automaticity. Other happenings may counteract, in some cases, the effect of mechanization on the original task. These involve changing the scope of the operator's duties.

Because less attention is required on a given machine, the operator may be given more machines to tend. He becomes responsible for manning a physically larger portion of the production sequence or a larger number of identical activities. As the worker becomes responsible for more machines, two types of effect are possible.

(*a*) He may be required to learn additional technical arts roughly on the same skill level as that which he previously possessed. For example, a milling-machine operator might be required to master a broaching machine and a drilling-tapping machine if they are integrated by automation in his work station. While these skills might not be more difficult or higher in degree, they definitely are additional requirements. Their inclusion in a worker's responsibility may or may not call for additional training. He may be required to learn an operation which involves a much higher degree of skill. I did not

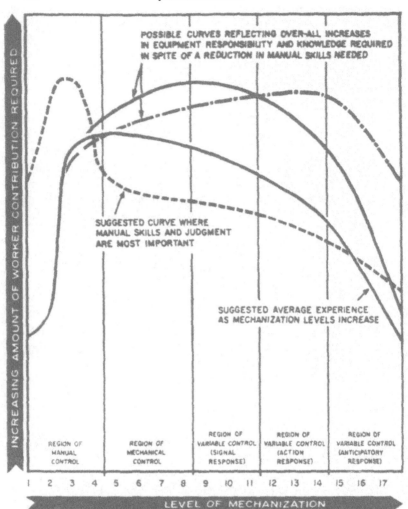

POSSIBLE CURVES REFLECTING OVER-ALL INCREASES
IN EQUIPMENT RESPONSIBILITY AND KNOWLEDGE REQUIRED
IN SPITE OF A REDUCTION IN MANUAL SKILLS NEEDED

SUGGESTED CURVE WHERE
MANUAL SKILLS AND JUDGMENT
ARE MOST IMPORTANT

SUGGESTED AVERAGE EXPERIENCE
AS MECHANIZATION LEVELS INCREASE

| REGION OF MANUAL CONTROL | REGION OF MECHANICAL CONTROL | REGION OF VARIABLE CONTROL (SIGNAL RESPONSE) | REGION OF VARIABLE CONTROL (ACTION RESPONSE) | REGION OF VARIABLE CONTROL (ANTICIPATORY RESPONSE) |

1   2   3   4   5   6   7   8   9   10   11   12   13   14   15   16   17

LEVEL OF MECHANIZATION

INCREASING AMOUNT OF WORKER CONTRIBUTION REQUIRED

CHART 5   How TOTAL CONTRIBUTION REQUIRED OF OPERATORS MAY
VARY WITH LEVELS OF MECHANIZATION

encounter many instances of this in my study. One example
was that of a master control board operator in a fertilizer
plant. Here semi-automatic control of the mixing activity
definitely involved more understanding, attention, and responsi-

bility on the part of this individual. Similarly, the growing complexity of the modern jet transport and its communications devices may require more training on the part of the pilot.

(b) In some automated jobs the demands on the operator for conventional duties are practically eliminated, but his new duties may embrace a portion of the set-up work or the inspection job. In other automated lines there may be no operator in the conventional sense. The individual responsible for this area of the production line may be a set-up man or an inspector.

To illustrate, I encountered an instance in which a maintenance worker was "manning" an automatic line. On another line where pistons were milled to weight automatically, the "operator" combined the remaining conventional operator duties with those of a set-up man—clearly an upgrading of the job.

The line between "set-up" and "operate" is a narrow one. In many industries an individual may perform the same set-up function as described above without requiring distinctly superior knowledge and training. Operators on some kinds of textile machinery are a good example. This source of job content increase may or may not be serious, but it is a possibility that we must recognize.

One upgrading effect of automation is to create new kinds of skilled jobs. These may require distinctly superior education, or demand significantly higher levels of comprehension and responsibility. Operators of master control panels may exemplify this trend as may computer programmers of complex problems.

Each of these happenings works in some way against the declining curves in Chart 5. We should not, however, jump to the conclusion that these types of conditions will always substantially upgrade the task or the total factory work force. The jobs just described do not seem to exist in any great number of industries or even in plants with a high overall level of mechanization. Often a highly mechanized factory will have only one control board job and, at the most, only a handful of such positions. Accordingly, the net effect of automation in most plants I have studied or read about was to reduce, or at least not to increase, the demand for skills and abilities on the part of the direct labour force.

Indirect labour. As automation displaces the machine operator, the line between direct and indirect labour becomes harder to distinguish. Has the operator become a set-up man or the set-up man an operator? Regardless of one's answer, an important skill change is evident in the set-up activity. Machine preparation and adjustment frequently are more complex, more difficult, and require a wider range of technical knowledge and competence. This is not only because of the complexity of the equipment, but even more to the intermingling of the five types of control systems— hydraulic, pneumatic, electrical, electronic, and mechanical. Also, work-feeding devices must be synchronized and otherwise regulated, and new degrees of precision must be obtained by careful adjustment.

The increased demands imposed on the set-up man are quite noticeable when a plant moves, for example, from level 5 of mechanization to level 12 or higher. On the other hand, if the old equipment already required a high degree of set-up skill (as on a conventional automobile engine-block line), then the move to automation probably does not increase the set-up man's skill and training requirements significantly. In a leading "automated" engine plant, for example, all job setters and their supervisors were given three hours of training in addition to the basic familiarization course given to the operators. Does this mean that there has been a distinct increase in the demand on job setters' knowledge?

Where indirect labour "mans" non-production-line machinery, such as power plants and materials-handling devices which are in themselves automated, the result is comparable to that for production-line machinery. The demand on the worker increases up to some point; then the spreading automaticity of the machinery generally begins to reduce this contribution in almost every respect.

To be sure, some new kinds of indirect labour jobs requiring a high degree of technical education may be created. An outstanding example is the introduction of numerically controlled machine tools. The programming of tapes initially required considerable technical education. These duties might be regarded as set-up jobs of very high calibre. It appeared that engineering or mathematical training would become the bare minimum education for the translation of desired results into programming instructions. This was the 1955–60 situation. But machine designers have progressed too. Now computerized tape production, through use of computer languages, is reducing this need.

In those plants that build their own automatic machinery there is a greater requirement for the peculiar talents needed for machinery development. Such cases are the main source of complaints about the shortage of adequately skilled people. Not only is technical training needed, but also some kind of skill in visualization, imagination, and mechanical creativity. Experienced managers have told me the latter is by no means obtainable simply by hiring more engineers. They point out that the real "skill" bottleneck in their factories is in the area of conceiving, designing, and building new machinery. The electrical engineering content is rising, as is the electronic content. Machinery builders and designers need more, and some distinctly higher skills.

Maintenance force. As I mentioned earlier, it is popularly assumed that maintenance will increase absolutely, or at least proportionally, under automation. Is it not obvious that the maintenance force will require a new order of skill?

The question cannot be answered with a simple "yes" or "no" because the maintenance force includes a number of kinds of skill, and these are not all equally affected by moves toward automation. For instance, I found no evidence that tinsmiths, pipe fitters, welders, and carpenters required increased skill; some evidence that hydraulic and pneumatic repairmen need better training because of the increased complexity of the control circuitry, and much evidence that a significant proportion of electricians needs rather complete retraining. The average plant electrician is no more prepared to cope with electronic circuitry than the average household

electrician is able to repair a TV set. It is a whole new
technical world, and it most definitely requires specialized
training in theory and practice. One major engine plant has
studied this problem and concluded that almost 2,000 hours
would be needed in class and shopwork to provide adequate
electronic training in addition to the firm's existing journeyman electrician training program of three years.

All of the plants I studied, employing even small amounts
of electronically controlled machinery, offered this same com-
plaint about maintenance skills. Frequently, the shortage was
so critical that it distorted attitudes toward the entire maintenance problem. Perhaps this is where part of society's trouble
in appraising automation lies. For instance; lack of electronic
maintenance skills was stated to be a critical problem in one
plant, and indeed was so. On closer examination, however, it
was found that not every electrician needed to have electronic
training. Of 700 men on maintenance, approximately 80 were
electricians, and the plant engineer estimated that he needed
just 3 or 4 competent electronic repairmen per shift. In other
words, only about 10 per cent of his electricians needed the
specialized skill and these amounted to only 1 per cent of his
total maintenance force. Such percentages do not make the
shortage less critical, but they suggest quite a different scale
of difficulty and a much smaller retraining problem. They also
suggest that we avoid loose statements which distort the
problem.

Automation also suggests the need for a new type of repair-
man: one competent in the five kinds of control circuitry that
we noted are involved. The reason for this new demand is
that it is too costly to send out a whole crew of repairmen or
to send a series of individual specialists each getting a little
bit further with the malfunctioning machine and finding that
his skill is not enough. The downtime implications of this
procedure are more than disturbing as the span of mechanization grows. Obtaining this kind of maintenance ability involves
a training problem and a union relations problem which few
managers have tackled, and fewer still have solved. I have
not heard of any major efforts by unions to provide this
integrated machine-repair skill.

Conclusion

In total, then, these limited observations and the theory offered here both suggest that increasing automation does not necessarily result in a new upgrading of work force skill requirements to a major extent. In fact, automation often tends to reduce the skill and training required on individual tasks.[9]

It is interesting to confirm these general conclusions by seeing what has been happening recently to the types of tasks that seemed to require higher skills.

Several firms have announced highly automatic machines in which set-up is performed by the push of a button or selection of a prepared tape. The numerically controlled Milwaukee Multimatic machine tool is an example. The set-up task is being mechanized to an important degree in some instances. Where this is so, the skills required by the set-up man are dropping.

M.I.T., I.B.M., and individual firms have developed English-like programming languages (APT and WALDO) for blue-print translation into computers. These enable the average draftsman in place of a numerically controlled tape programmer, to prepare many of his own computer instructions for the production of numerical control tapes. The educational and special training requirement is dropping.

It is also clear that mechanization and simplification of the maintenance task are occurring. The net effect of these two developments still seems to be minor because of a more rapid increase in the complexity of the automated equipment; and because of the growing amount of mechanization per production system. Still, the theory of skill *versus* automation proposed here is confirmed.

Numerous studies have suggested that routine operation of the computer, and even programming, do not require the high order of skill and training anticipated in the mid 1950's. The public schools in many communities have begun to train

[9]Note, however, that I have not attempted to deal with the increased demand for engineers and other technologists required to support the machine-building and control-building industries as the demand for automaticity grows. There may be serious skill shortages here, but they are hardly a part of the automation user's problem.

high school students to program computers. Progress in the
design of programs has greatly simplified programming.

The manufacture of certain new products suggests that a
new trend will spread into parts of industry, and will affect
the calibre of "skill" required by the worker. This trend is
evident in at least two industries—the manufacture of computers and defense-astronautics equipment. Yet here we have
two booming industries characterized by extremely complex
products, and continuous technological change involving much
research and development. The number of units of any one
model produced is very small—frequently only one—and the
cost of each unit is very high—frequently in the tens of millions
of dollars. Highly precise manufacturing and assembly are
required, and the need for reliability is so great that testing
and check-out are major "production" tasks. This kind of manufacturing requires a work force with a high proportion of
technically trained people, ranging from applied scientists
through test engineers and master machinists. Thus the "skill"
of the total work force requires drastic upgrading. Note, however, that this need for skill results from the nature of the
product, not from the manufacturing technique. It also occurs
because the amount of automation employed in manufacturing
is less than normal; and not because its effects are different
from those suggested in this paper.

WAGE DETERMINATION

It is not enough for management simply to be aware of the
possible effects of automation on its work force. We are left
with a dilemma. What should be done about compensation?
We have seen that both theoretically and practically some
downgrading seems to occur, as does some upgrading; yet
effects are badly mixed from job to job, system to system,
industry to industry, and even from time to time. Thus major
problems in job evaluation, wage administration, and contract
negotiations are created.

The wage problem can be expressed simply. If the operator
does not control quantity and quality; if he makes fewer pro-

duction operation decisions; if he exerts less physical and mental effort; if automation reduces the need for skill, education, and experience; if automation removes job hazards and improves working conditions; then many traditional worker contributions are of lesser or even of no economic value. What, therefore, should be the criteria for wages? Should the employee be paid less because he contributes less, or the same because of the unfortunate implications of reduction, or more because of increased productivity? If more, how much and on what basis?

The possibilities that have been suggested can be grouped loosely as follows:

1. Employees working with the automated machinery should get a share of the increased productivity. The division could be handled in any one of the following ways: (a) The firm should simply split the gain in output and increase wages proportionately as if they were piece-rate gains. (b) There should be a "reasonable" increase—five cents per hour, or 10 per cent of present take-home pay, or some other stipulated amount (very vague bases for the amount have been offered). (c) Each increase should be negotiated with the union with due regard for the individual situation. Many firms felt that this was very bad policy since it had potentials for costly negotiations, ill will, and bickering. (d) The increase should not be specific by incident but part of an annual wage-improvement program applicable to all employees. Such a policy forces management to keep improving productivity. It offers a certainty for wage gains to all the labour force, and it reduces endless negotiating sessions. (e) The increase should be that called for by the job evaluation system. Usually the firms felt that no decreases should be applied even though indicated.

2. There should be neither specific increases nor productivity clause increases, but rather all such gains should be regarded as reserves out of which wage increases can be made at "appropriate" times.

3. The gains of automation other than those requiring additional contribution by the worker belong to the firm. Since the company has provided the capital and the planning, the

benefits should be directed towards the long-range welfare of the business. In the long run, this is to the employee's best interest for he may benefit more if prices are reduced or if the business is expanded or reserves set aside for a rainy day.

4. One union claim has been: "These new classifications and rates should be established in recognition of the changed nature of jobs in which increased responsibility offsets by far any reduction in physical effort and manual dexterity accompanying automation. This increased responsibility, in most cases, flows from the much larger investment represented by the equipment under the individual worker's control. . . ."[10] This claim should be examined carefully, since it is not necessarily true. The worker may have more responsibility if the equipment literally is under his control. However, automation ultimately takes control out of the worker's hands, in both the literal and figurative sense. Future wage agreements based on this "control" claim should be very carefully worded, therefore, or managers and unions will find that they have established some embarrassing and confusing policies.

Notice also the claim that responsibility is measured by investment. Payment for responsibility where investment is the yardstick is loaded with inequities for the non-automated work force. Tool and die makers would lose pay status enormously, as also would maintenance men. The investment basis would upset existing wage structures and would be grossly unfair to those less mechanized operators whose duties truly require more skill, training, and other contributions.

However, responsibility may be increased because of dependence on the operator's alertness and intelligence in preventing a machinery stoppage involving a large portion of the productive capacity, safety, or in rapidly restoring operating conditions. This easily could override all other considerations and justify substantial additional compensation. Yet we should anticipate that eventually automatic controls will be introduced to provide this "responsibility" function too, reduc-

[10]*Automation* (Detroit: UAW-CIO Education Department, 1955), pp. 16–17.

ing or eliminating even this operator contribution. "Responsibility" is a dubious quality on which to establish wages.

With this understanding of the relationship between automation and skill let us review some trends in wage determination as affected by automation. It is obvious that in negotiations between labour and management "automation" is used as a synonym for general technological progress, and not to mean just automatic machinery. As of 1965 there are some identifiable effects of automation in wage determination which will be briefly discussed.

Annual Productivity Increases

"Automation" as a word has been deliberately avoided by many managers and engineers as personal policy, and by some major firms as corporate policy. They regard the term as inflammatory, misleading, and inaccurate. They (and some others who do use the term) recognize that automation is not a new phenomenon and, to varying degrees, that increased output per worker can flow from sources other than automatic equipment (such as changes in plant layout or an increase in the power or speed of existing types of equipment). Therefore, special recognition of automation alone is both foolish and incorrect.

The answer, some say, is in a contract providing labour with an annual productivity increase. General Motors Corporation and the United Automobile Workers have applied this concept with great success, I believe, and without government intervention.

From the union viewpoint, an annual or periodic percentage increase assures all workers of some benefits from technological progress. It assures them of a wage increase on schedule, and without endless bargaining over hundreds of individual jobs. It also assures them of a wage increase whether or not individual managers are smart or aggressive in improving methods. Presumably it should encourage top management to be vigorous in improving methods and remaining competitive, and thus protect the majority of the union jobs.

From the management viewpoint it has the advantage of reducing endless negotiations on individual jobs. It allows effort at improvement to be expended where and when management chooses, and it encourages each member of management toward constant effort to improve.

The annual wage increase was introduced in the 1948 and 1950 GM-UAW Agreements before "automation" was a widely recognized word.[11] Nevertheless, "technical progress, better tools, methods, processes and equipment" were recognized in Article 101 (*a*) in the 1950 Agreement as a source or "continuing improvement in the standard of living." The "annual improvement factor" in effect, covered and still covers wage adjustments for "automation."

Automation Funds

This trend is a recent formal recognition of an old idea: that management and labour should establish a fund which is created by contributions of money related to changes in equipment or methods resulting in greater output per man-hour and from which money is disbursed to share the gains with retained workers, and/or to study the best means of accomplishing these purposes.

The United Mine Workers Welfare and Retirement Fund was launched in May, 1946 by agreement between the Union and Julius Krug, Secretary of the Interior under President Truman, during a period of strike when the U.S. government had seized the mines. It began with a contribution of five cents per ton of coal mined. As of 1960, the fund collected on about 77.5 per cent of all coal produced in the United States (some mines are not unionized; others are in default). By 1965 the results had come under serious criticism. The number of workers employed in coal mining has dropped by many thousands. Many small mines have been forced to close because they cannot pay union wages and cannot afford the large investments required for highly mechanized mining.

[11]"Automation" first appeared as a word in public print in *American Machinist*, vol. 92, no. 22, Oct. 21, 1948, pp. 107–22. The word was originated by D. S. Harder of the Ford Motor Company.

Other funds have followed. We might note the West Coast Longshore Fund, established in 1959 specifically over the issue of mechanization, which was further modified in 1960 to a Mechanization and Modernization Fund, involving the employers payment of a flat fee of $5 million per year for five years. Professor Thomas Kennedy, my colleague at Harvard Business School, gives many details on these funds in his scholarly and comprehensive book, *Automation Funds and Displaced Workers*[12] which should be carefully studied by everyone interested in wage negotiations. From this book I draw these major conclusions: (*a*) The use of automation funds probably will grow in American labour negotiations. (*b*) The goals of automation funds vary widely from fund to fund. (*c*) The benefits of automation funds are astonishingly diverse. (*d*) Present national and state legislation in the United States specifically restrict certain kinds of benefits and payments from automation funds. Existing legislation must be carefully studied before defining the methods of payment in establishing such funds. (*f*) Methods of financing automation funds are quite diverse. (*g*) The method of financing the automation fund greatly changes the flow of funds under various conditions. Professor Kennedy offers four charts showing how twelve methods of financing affect total fund income, annual fund income per employee, fund income per hour worked, and fund income as a percentage of average employee earnings under four combinations of automation expansion-stability-decline. These charts deserve critical consideration, since they show widely different effects. (*h*) Most vital is the effect of the method of financing on management's incentive to automate, and on employees' incentive to co-operate. No one can read Professor Kennedy's book without realizing that an automation fund is very tricky business for both management and labour. This field deserves continued attention, since the idea probably will spread.

A growing feature of many contracts not built around automation funds is the retraining provision (exemplified in the Armour Fund of the early 1960's). Major contracts in meat

[12]Boston: Harvard Business School, Division of Research, 1962.

packing, communications, printing, steelmaking, and railroad operations now include a variety of provisions along the lines of company financed training for new, high skill jobs, seniority for training on new jobs, and company-union financed study teams on retraining problems.

Automation Job Loss Agreements

There are many collective-bargaining agreements that attempt to permit, facilitate, or encourage technological change by gearing new equipment and methods to normal attrition rates. More and more agreements specify that no worker shall lose his job as a result of technological change—this despite the obvious fact that it is difficult sometimes to distinguish between job losses as a result of technological change and those resulting from shifts in demand, in product design, or product mix.

By 1960 many union-company agreements contained references to "automation," and included some provisions as to the job protection, and seniority rights that would be given to affected workers. Job protection was also a major issue to certain declining industries. This was dramatized throughout the United States by the findings of the President's independent study commission on railroad practices. In effect, the commissioners agreed with railroad management's contention that certain traditional work practices, such as firemen on diesel locomotives, were unnecesary. The report recommended that the railroads should be free to make work-rule changes and to mechanize and modernize.

This finding threatened, and still does threaten an already troubled industry with wholesale job losses. The railway unions instigated various legal manoeuvers to delay action or to nullify the commission's findings. In 1962, a month-long strike of telegraphers against the Chicago & Northwestern Railway brought the issue to a head. Shall firms in this industry be allowed to mechanize and modernize on a wholesale basis that will result in thousands of job losses? The railroads said they must, in order to survive as a healthy transportation industry. The unions said the usual things about mass displacement.

The strike was settled by the binding decision of a special arbitration panel, which held that the railroad had the right to drop telegraphers' jobs without prior union warning.

Many more railroad situations were brought closer to a management-labour deadlock by the trend of following events. In May 1963 the Brotherhood of Railway Clerks and the Southern Pacific Company signed a landmark agreement which ended a major strike threat. It provided 11,000 clerks with almost complete protection against displacement by automation and it gave the railroad the right to gradual improvement. The railroad agreed that jobs within the union's jurisdiction would be eliminated only by natural attrition—death, discharge with cause, or retirement. The agreement has the unique feature of allowing the railroad to eliminate a union job other than the one specifically vacated. However, the eliminated worker can claim any other job through seniority. If he has insufficient seniority, the company can discharge him, but he receives 70 per cent of his pay for one year and 60 per cent for an additional four years. He is also entitled to job retraining under a railroad-federal government program. These wage benefits also are applicable to 4000 men discharged since 1958 who remained on call for employment.

Since the railroad can eliminate the position represented by any union clerk who leaves the work force, or can shift its vacancy "credits" to selected areas (for a price), a gradual program of reduction is insured. Yet automation can be applied in promising areas and the worker is protected from arbitrary displacement without compensation and retraining. Doubtless this settlement will establish the direction of some future automation agreements.

Portable Pensions, Preferential Employment, and Broadened Seniority Rights

Partly because of automation, partly because of the technological displacement of one defence industry by another (e.g., the missile displacing the airplane), there has been great interest in protection of vested interests for displaced workers. Some proposals suggest industry-wide "portability" of job benefits. Others have suggested nation-wide portability. At this writing, no industry-wide programs have been introduced, but the concept is receiving increasing attention. Preferential employment rights—meaning that when one plant of a company closes down the displaced worker shall have priority at other company plants for a limited period—are appearing in some contracts. Whether this is the effect of automation may be doubtful, but the idea is spreading and has been suggested as an industry-wide concept. Broadening seniority rights are in evidence in current contracts. This is especially important since automation may destroy job skills and whole departments. Plant-wide and even company-wide seniority programs exist. Lockheed, for instance, even provides moving allowances to workers. Again this is not solely a result of automation, but represents the technological displacement at work in whole industries.

Job Evaluation Problems

In 1958 and 1960 I raised the question whether job evaluation would be an effective way to determine proper wages on automated jobs. I hypothesized that it would not be satisfactory because, first, according to the theory of mechanization levels and their effect on worker contributions, and as reinforced by observations in some automated plants, it was clear that in many, and possibly most, instances the total contribution by the worker was less than before automation. This leaves us with a factual situation that workers, unions, society in general, and even some managers, are emotionally or socially unable to accept; namely, that automation generally calls for downward wage revisions. Secondly, job evaluation systems distribute points for skill, education, and other contributions in weightings appropriate to the operator contributions using existing machinery. However, the effect of automation or progress toward automation usually is to shift the relative importance of these factors, even eliminating some of them such as physical effort or manual skill. Thus the old point scale, and even the factors included, are utterly inappropriate to the new jobs. Thirdly, most factories are mixtures of conventional and automated activities. If additional job evaluation systems were developed for the automated jobs, the firm would then have to use two (or more) evaluation systems. This has great potential for endless confusion, bickering, and injustice.

I have seen nothing in automation progress or in job evaluation activities to alter these hypotheses of five years ago. S. Herbert Unterberger, one of America's leading professional arbitrators, reported to his associates at their annual meeting in January, 1963, that a recent review of the literature failed to reveal any published exploration on the development of job evaluation systems for automation.

Mr. Unterberger's interesting and useful paper deals with problems of the arbitrator attempting to settle job evaluation problems in "automated" jobs.[13] He said, ". . . the measuring devices used in most current job evaluation plans . . . involve a series of implied assumptions which are not appropriate for the measurement of automated jobs. The most serious of these is the assumption that skill is the key factor in determining the value of a job, as indicated by the fact that the skill factors generally receive half or more of the weight. . . ." Mr. Unterberger then makes some penetrating suggestions which I sum up here as follows:

Arbitrators of today should be as creative as their predecessors who dealt with the beginnings of job evaluation systems in the 1920's. Specifically, when evaluating the new types of jobs they should recognize, point out to the parties concerned, and consider in their decisions, the new characteristics. Of course, this can only be done as permitted by the legal agreement under which he is charged to operate.

The new characteristics of some jobs, but by no means all, are, a need for alertness and attentiveness; ability to accept supervision at long range, perhaps through written instead of oral communication; isolation, which in addition to the possibility of boredom, may allow less opportunity to learn from one's fellows, and therefore require greater preparatory training; and tension, because of responsibility for greater output.

[13]"*Automation and Job Evaluation Techniques,*" *1963 Proceedings of the National Academy of Arbitrators.*

He suggests that where a general evaluation of various jobs in the labour market is the guiding principle, as in a job-to-job comparison system, the labour market's evaluation of the highly automated job may be appropriate, but no final guidance.

Finally, he identifies a major problem in transitional jobs. While automation is being installed and debugged, very difficult and hazardous conditions may exist. The operator may need an exceptional amount of education and experience, and a very high premium may be placed upon his sense of responsibility, his alertness and judgment, his effective imagination, and intuition. After the system is debugged, reliability enhanced, and perhaps special trouble indication or correction devices installed, there will be a startling drop in worker contributions. The need for everyone of these valuable qualities may be literally eliminated. At what point, then, shall a permanent rate be placed on the job?

Unterberger describes one job in which the trouble shooting continued for over two years, with the Union contending that the job should be evaluated and a rate set, while the company wanted to wait until the system had been perfected. His conclusion is that an evaluation correct for the transition period is very likely to be in great error for the long run. Hence, extreme care is essential if we are not to discourage progress, and even a firm's effort to remain competitive. To this I would add that management and labour be especially careful in rate setting on pioneer jobs that establish industry patterns. An excessive rate may seriously retard national industrial progress; or it may prove to be at odds with the true worth of the job that it disrupts the rest of a carefully prepared and well accepted wage structure.

My opinion is that it may be useful to establish a "start-up" or "debugging" rate, which would fairly compensate the worker during the transition period of excessive job effort. However, will debugging then ever cease? I can also visualize the alternative of a small class of employees whose job title was "start-up man" and who would turn over jobs to regular employees only when the equipment was debugged. Only the largest firms could use such men continuously. Another possibility might be a special assignment and duty category for maintenance men as "start-up men."

Another study bearing on the job evaluation question, "The Effects of Technological Change Upon Job Content" by Ronald Jablonski,[14] examines changes in job content in the United States steel industry between 1950 and 1962, and concludes that there was a rise in "job class" (as defined by the steel industries job evaluation system) of about one job class (from all causes) in these twelve years. Of the 80″ computer-controlled, automatic hot strip mill and the continuous annealer then under construction, the author said that, ". . . both indicated that a level of control is being approached where the changes in job content begin to level off and decline." The job evaluation system still "works" because job content has been moving up as mechanization has moved up through, say, levels 10 and 11 (on our Chart 1). Also, it works because "skill" accounts for less than one-fourth of the steel industry's job evaluation points, in contrast to the 50 per cent or more for skill in most job evaluation scales. Therefore, the steel industry's scale is inherently better adapted to dealing with automation. But, the author's comments with respect to the 80″ mill: ". . . Most of the factors have their rating governed by conditions during the roll changing operation, or by the fact that some rolling in annually is required. Thus one has the feeling that these jobs are somewhat overrated relative to those on a manually operated mill . . . Perhaps what is needed is a system wherein one set of ratings will apply during automatic operations and another set during manual operations and set-up."

Finally, Jablonski offered a new problem. When programmed control systems are applied in a firm, and when the crew is expected to operate the system manually at peak capacity, in event of breakdown, the crew must acquire its full range of conventional skills. Shall they be compensated for skills needed during normal operation or emergency operation?

[14]Unpublished doctoral thesis submitted in May, 1963, to the faculty of the Graduate School of Business Administration, Harvard University.

Or for the time of actually using those respective skills? His tentative opinion is that workers should be compensated for peak skill needed, regardless of the amount of application. This is, he says, the basis of compensating other craftsmen and professionals such as doctors or lawers. As of September 1965, there was growing evidence that the steel industry was indeed reaching the condition anticipated by Jablonski.

Incentive Systems

It is sometimes stated that automation means the end of incentive systems. The worker cannot control pace or quality, so how can an incentive system be applied?

In a number of individual cases (mostly non-union), management and workers have simply dropped the piece-rate incentive, and given the workers some sort of increase—five cents per hour, 10 per cent average. Some unions have argued for a piece-rate increase of one-half of the increase in output. Obviously, either approach is simply an agreement without a measured basis, although it may be quite useful as a basis for collective bargaining.

A little thought and research shows that it is not true that incentives are ended under automation. The textile industry is a highly automated process, yet it finds incentives very useful. These incentives, however, are placed on something other than pieces of output, and are intended to achieve a different purpose. The traditional incentive is a bonus for exceeding a personal norm of output. It is a share of the output of extraordinary skill or expenditure of effort. The essential notion is, "produce more and we will reward you proportionally." It recognizes labour as a major cost of production. In the textile industry, incentives are paid on the basis of maintaining or exceeding a certain machine utilization. This incentive recognizes that the worker cannot personally exert effort to produce a norm. The machine sets the norm through its normal operating speed. However, the worker can help to minimize failures to achieve the norm. The more common detractions are: machine breakdown; faulty output due to malfunction, resulting in scrap; faulty input, meaning delay, or generation of scrap; slow material delivery or work feeding; and, clumsy procedures and delays in set-up, servicing and trouble shooting.

I believe that in many extreme cases it will be highly desirable to pay incentives based upon maintaining a specified machine utilization. This incentive program recognizes the fixed cost of production, and encourages labour to help management minimize machinery non-performance. A logical outgrowth of this is the crew incentive, which would recognize the group contribution toward effective use of facilities. Most plant-wide plans grant a percentage of the increase in profits.

The Kaiser Pact

In January 1963, the Kaiser Steel Corporation signed an unusual agreement with its employees; a company-wide incentive plan granting a percentage of production cost savings. It also includes some protection against automation. Major features are:

1. Employees shall receive 32.5 per cent of future savings in materials, supplies, and labour required to produce finished steel. Capital expenditures on existing facilities to reduce cost shall be deducted, but capital investments in increased capacity or new processes will not be deducted.

2. A base period will be chosen on which savings will be calculated monthly and audited annually by a firm of Chartered Public Accountants.

3. Workers whose jobs are eliminated by automation will go into a labour pool and be paid at old job rates for at least the average hours worked per week until openings are available. (Employment reserve.)

4. Any worker missing promotions or hours of work because of technological improvements will be entitled to average hourly pay for a year or more. These payments will be deducted from the cost savings to be shared. (Income security.)

This pact was hailed by the union and bitterly criticized by some other steel company executives. They pointed out that it commits Kaiser to pay extra labour costs even if the company is operating at a loss. They also deplored the idea of the union "look at the books."

The end results of this contract are not yet apparent. Profit-sharing payments were first made in May 1963. In the first year workers received 53¢ per hour worked (an average of $850); in the second year 39¢ per hour worked; and in the third year (not yet completed) 46¢ per hour worked. The automation job loss protection features have not been widely tested because of the growing volume of business. In the first fifteen months 69 jobs were provided through the employment reserve feature, and 207 jobs received income security when displaced to lower paying jobs.

CONCLUSION

Automation, has, in the United States, highlighted several things other than wage determination. Seniority, for instance, is becoming a less useful labour concept because it is less needed, and is less applicable. Most significant is the federal government's notice of automation. Since 1955, there have been at least four Congressional Hearings on automation and related problems. President Kennedy held one White House Conference on automation to expose viewpoints in the area. Numerous government sponsored special committees and tripartite investigating and advisory groups have included effects of automation in their assignments.[15]

It seems that the ultimate effect of automation on wage determination is to highlight the need for job security combined with the encouragement of technological progress. Many of the charges against, and the claims for, automation are ridiculous. Automation, as a social issue, is gradually bringing to all people a realization that no nation can be stable and happy if its work force is insecure; and that no nation can build a rewarding society for increasing numbers unless it employs automation and technological advances. Automation is destroy-

[15]The latest and presumably most comprehensive is the Report of the National Commission on Technology, Automation, and Economic Progress, *Technology and the American Economy*, vol. 1, Feb. 1966.

ing the usefulness and validity of many old forms of labour payment, while technological change, including automation, is also shifting the location of work in the plant, and occasionally even in the country.

I believe that automation will ultimately push us toward a salaried industrial society. And, I suggest that if we are wise and effective in developing moral standards of honest workmanship and values of professional pride in all employees, the salaried society with moderate, but definitely not absolute, job security, offers democracy and mankind its happiest industrial environment.

The most serious problem seems to be that the gradual application of automation, plus the factors affecting annual productivity increases, are substantially reducing the percentage of labour cost in the manufacturing total. Figures of 15, 11, and even 7 per cent can be found in some mass production firms. Increased demand for traditional products will not absorb all of the labour surplus. Demand for new products will help and a shift of employment to service industries may ultimately be the source of more jobs.

The second problem is only a personal reaction, but I deplore the loss of manual skill (not heavy physical effort) and the element of craftsmanship in work. It seems to me that automation is destroying this basic source of job satisfaction. I would not turn back the technological clock, but I believe society is losing something of great value when craftsmanship disappears.

As for immediate, wholesale displacement of workers— automation is a trifling threat compared to the technological battle between industries. The missile *versus* the manned aircraft is a dramatic forerunner of a coming growing difficulty for labour and management. By far the most serious problem on the horizon is this wholesale displacement of an industry or service by technologically superior development. This is coming with increasing speed and severity. It will require great mutual understanding and adjustment between labour, management, and government.

3

Collective Bargaining in Perspective

FREDERICK HARBISON*

COLLECTIVE BARGAINING is now so well entrenched and widely accepted that people are beginning to suggest that it is becoming obsolete. For example, Paul Jacobs claims that collective bargaining has become "old before its time." He says that it has proved less and less effective in solving the basic problems faced by workers and management, and points out that an increasing number of workers remain outside the system and are not likely ever to come within it.[1] Others lament the encroachment by government into the area of free bargaining between unions and management. The noted British labour economist, Ben Roberts, recently stated that the refutation of *laissez-faire* collective bargaining is quite widely accepted by all political parties in Britain, as well as in advanced and underdeveloped nations. He says, for example:[2]

In many European countries it has been found necessary to contain collective bargaining within the general framework of a national incomes policy. It appears that in these countries a consensus has been reached that the outcome of "free" collective

---

*Director, Industrial Relations Section, Princeton University.

[1]Paul Jacobs, *Old before Its Time: Collective Bargaining at 28* (Santa Barbara, Calif.: Center for Study of Democratic Institutions, 1963).

[2]Comments by B. C. Roberts in session "Is the American System of Collective Bargaining Obsolete?" Industrial Relations Research Association, Dec. 1964. See IRRA, *Proceedings of 17th Annual Meeting*, p. 160.

bargaining is not, in most cases, in the best interests of all . . . collective bargaining, in and by itself, is not a device that promotes general economic equity and cannot be relied upon for purposes of economic stability.

These statements miss the mark. Collective bargaining, in my judgment, is not becoming obsolete; it is a vital and constructive force in an enterprise economy. Those who cling to the obsolescence concept, I think, may have a distorted view of the essential functions of bargaining in our society, because they expect it to solve problems which lie far beyond its practical reach.

In this paper I propose to examine the essential characteristics of collective bargaining, the impact of collective bargaining in an enterprise economy, and the limitations of collective bargaining in economies such as in the United States and Canada.

THE ESSENTIAL CHARACTERISTICS OF COLLECTIVE BARGAINING

First, collective bargaining is strictly a relationship between organizations. Contrary to a mistaken belief in many quarters, collective bargaining is not a relationship between management and workers. Management-employee relations encompass direct dealings between company officials and workers as individuals, whereas collective bargaining is confined to dealings between company spokesmen and the representatives of the union which is the bargaining agency of the employees.

Second, collective bargaining is a power relationship between organizations. *Bona fide* collective bargaining does not exist unless the union has the ultimate right to resort to force, in the form of a strike, and unless the representatives of management also have the ultimate right to refuse workers employment if they are unwilling to acquiesce to the demands of the union. Stated more bluntly, collective bargaining does not exist unless each party is free to negotiate with a club which is within handy reach in case of necessity. In this relationship, the all-embracing and legitimate objective of the union is to put pressure on the employer—pressure for wages and other benefits, pressure to protect the jobs and employment rights of the members, and pressure to limit the unilateral exercise by management of its prerogatives. Union leaders are the advocates, "the Philadelphia lawyers" so to speak, of the members, and at the same time they are policemen hired to provide protection for the members from the daily exercise of unilateral managerial authority in the shop. The all-embracing and legitimate objective of management, of course, is to resist this pressure—to fight for retention of essential managerial rights, to keep from losing its shirt by making unwarranted concessions, and thus to safeguard the well-being and profitability of the enterprise. Collective bargaining, therefore, is a pressure-generating process, and those who engage in it must recognize quite frankly that they operate in "the squeeze-box."

Third, collective bargaining is essentially a treaty-making and treaty-enforcing process between companies and unions. The end objective of collective bargaining is to arrive at a mutually satisfactory contract setting forth, for a period of time, agreements on such things as wages, hours, and other conditions of employment. During the period when the contract is in force, the principal activity of the parties is the administration and interpretation of its provisions. In well-established collective relations this treaty-administering function is customarily performed in a very orderly manner.

Finally, collective bargaining is in practice a process of accommodation between companies and unions. Although open conflict and guerrilla warfare may be characteristic of some relationships at particular points of time, the vast majority of collective relationships provides an avenue for orderly and peaceful resolution of differences through compromise, agreement, and co-operation. Thus, despite the fact that collective bargaining has its roots in a conflict of interests between capital and labour and cannot exist without the right of both parties ultimately to back up their respective interests with force, it is really an instrument for furthering industrial peace. It is a way of organizing divergent interests in such a way as to resolve rather than to extend open conflict.

The collective-bargaining process can be greatly improved if the parties take a rational, unemotional, and sophisticated view of it. There can be constructive responses to pressure. For example, there is today a great deal of interest in "creative collective bargaining." A growing number of companies and unions have made considerable progress in establishing joint study committees, "continuous negotiation" procedures, effective use of impartial neutrals, and the use of permanent arbitrators. The Kaiser experience, the Human Relations Committee in the basic steel industry, the Armour Automation Committee, and the Mechanization and Modernization Agreement in the West Coast Longshore Industry are illustrative of attempts, with varying degrees of success, to introduce more business-like rationality into bargaining relationships.[3] These and similar efforts to develop greater understanding of critical issues can result in smoother operation of bargaining even though it still must take place within a pressure-generating framework.

Name-calling, bargaining in the newspapers, guerrilla tactics, accusations, and emotional outbursts need not be part of the pressure-generating process; rather they are manifestations of immature, unsophisticated, and unskilled bargaining which is becoming obsolete. Bargaining is a business for professionals, not amateurs, and can be improved by more objective consideration of facts, more effective selection and better training of bargainers, and more realism in taking and holding positions. Power relationships by no means imply a concentration on the use of the weapons of industrial warfare.

THE IMPACT OF COLLECTIVE BARGAINING

Is collective bargaining "a good thing"? Is it a constructive or destructive force in our kind of economy?

I would argue that collective bargaining, where it operates with reasonable success, fulfils four major functions: first, it provides a partial means for resolving the conflicting economic interests of management and labour; second, it greatly enhances

[3]For descriptive analysis of some of these, see James J. Healy and James A. Henderson, *Creative Collective Bargaining* (Englewood Cliffs, N.J.: Prentice-Hall, 1965).

the rights, dignity, and worth of workers as industrial citizens; and, third, as a consequence of the first two functions, it provides one of the more important bulwarks for the preservation of the private-enterprise system. And finally, it provides a measure of industrial peace.

On behalf of its members, the union demands wage increases, vacations with pay, pensions, sickness benefits, and many other things which workers want. In practically all collective-bargaining treaties, agreement on these matters is reached, the final settlement usually being somewhere between what the union asks for and what the employer at the outset says he is willing to give. When the contract is finally signed, the union leadership usually takes pains to point out that the new terms and conditions of employment represent a victory for the workers. Thus most workers in organized plants probably feel that the union has pushed the employer about as far as he will go. Management customarily indicates that, although the concessions have been perhaps too costly, it will try to get along somehow. For all practical purposes, then, these economic issues are resolved for periods varying from perhaps six months to as much as five years. Provision is made, furthermore, for the orderly settlement of individual grievances over wage rates and employment rights during the life of the contract. From the standpoint of the workers, this method of getting commitments from management on wages and working conditions is much more satisfying than being forced to rely on managerial discretion on such matters. Management can also breathe more easily knowing that these issues are more or less settled for the time being. On the part of both parties, therefore, there is usually a sense of satisfaction in concluding by mutual agreement a treaty which gives each a feeling of security, if not a sense of achievement.

The economic impact of these bargains on individual firms and on the economy as a whole, however, is an entirely separate question. Economists as yet have not been able to resolve their differences, either in theory or in fact, on the impact of the union. For example, the late Henry Simons and his followers would argue that unions possess almost unlimited monopoly power and succeed in benefiting their members only at the expense of the unorganized groups in society. They would also contend that collective bargaining, in exerting an upward pressure on wages, must inevitably result either in price inflation or in general unemployment.[4] Yet other economists tend to discount the effect of unions on wages, on allocation of resources, and on general levels of prices and employment. Milton Friedman, for example, has stated that the long-run effect of unions on the structure and level of wage rates and, thereby, on the allocation of economic resources is of minor magnitude in comparison with other economic forces.[5] The empirical evidence in this area is quite scanty and as yet does not provide sufficient evidence to prove either of these contentions. Thus the "jury of economists" weighing the economic impact of the union is hung.

I would agree with George Hildebrand that collective bargaining has not captured wages at the expense of profits, and has not greatly disturbed relative wages and the distribution of labour. Nor has it impeded economic growth. Its economic impact has been minor. Certainly, we would not expect union pressure on management to increase productivity, to improve efficiency, or to make enterprises more profitable. Unions in our part of the world are management regulating devices; they are not expected, as in the communist countries, to energize workers in the production process. In enterprise economies, this is the job of good management. To be sure, without regulation by unions through the process of collective bargaining, management might be able to increase production standards slightly, to introduce new methods and machinery a little bit more rapidly, to reduce working forces a little bit more easily, and thus perhaps to operate enterprises a little more efficiently from a strictly economic point of view. Let us

[4]See, in particular, Henry C. Simons, "Some Reflections on Syndicalism," *Journal of Political Economy*, March, 1944; and Charles E. Lindblom, *Unions and Capitalism* (New Haven: Yale University Press, 1949).

[5]Milton Friedman, "Some Comments on the Significance of Labor Unions for Economic Policy," in David McCord Wright, ed., *The Impact of the Union* (New York: Harcourt Brace, 1951), chap. 10.

concede, then, that the economic impact of unions may be slightly negative. Speaking as a professor, I might give collective bargaining a slightly failing grade in the economic area, but this would be a marginal decision.

The evaluation of the consequences of collective bargaining on the rights, dignity and worth of workers as industrial citizens, however, is another matter. In the unionized plants the collective agreement establishes the framework of a system of industrial jurisprudence. It defines the rights of individuals and groups, and it provides machinery for the adjudication of grievances. At every turn, moreover, collective bargaining forces management to take cognizance of the effect of its decisions on the rights and interests of workers. If management decides to introduce new methods and machinery, for example, it must carefully weigh the impact of such changes on the workers involved. Or, if it wants to promote an employee to a higher position out of line of seniority, it must be absolutely certain that the individual involved has superior ability and competence. In short, the mere existence of a collective-bargaining relationship, quite apart from the specific clauses in the contract, puts continuous pressure on the employer to eliminate causes of employee discontent and to think in terms of human values in the management of people. One of the most striking features of our system of industrial relations is the energetic response of employers to actual or potential union pressure. This pressure often leads to programs for better selection and placement of employees, improved foreman-training programs, better systems of wage and salary administration, and more effective two-way communication between management and workers. Such positive responses may be even more prevalent in the unorganized establishments than in unionized plants, for in such cases management often bends over backward to treat employees decently if for no other reason than to prevent them from bringing a union into the plant.

Thus the collective-bargaining contract establishes the body of law, and the union provides the police force for protection and extension of employees' rights on the job. To be sure, this system is not without its defects and drawbacks. First, some labour leaders, as they become securely entrenched in their unions, tend to lose touch with the rank and file and to become insensitive to the complaints and desires of the people they are supposed to represent. Second, some types of rigid working rules and regulations prescribed by contract may be as distasteful to some workers as unilateral managerial authority. Third, in rare instances, management and labour bureaucrats may conclude "sweetheart agreements" which completely ignore the fundamental interests of workers. Yet few persons would deny that, on the whole, the direct and indirect consequence of collective bargaining is to bring about more consideration for the freedom, dignity, and worth of the working men and women in modern industrial society. Here, I think, collective bargaining can be given a very high grade. Its impact, on the whole, is clearly constructive and positive.

I would also give collective bargaining another high grade for its role as a bulwark of the private enterprise system. To the extent that collective bargaining operates successfully as an orderly means of resolving the conflicting economic interests of management and labour and to the extent that it enhances the dignity and worth of labourers in their role as factors of production, it provides some very substantial support for our system of democratic capitalism. It does this by providing a drainage channel for the specific dissatisfactions and frustrations which workers experience on the job, by helping to "humanize" the operation of an essentially impersonal price system by making it more generally acceptable to workers as a group, and, by absorbing the energies and interests of the leaders of labour who might be inclined to work for the overthrow of capitalism if this avenue of activity were lacking.

The operation of collective bargaining as a drainage channel for worker dissatisfactions is so obvious as hardly to warrant further elaboration. In this country day-to-day union-management relationships centre on problems arising at the bench. The average local union leader spends most of his time listening to complaints and settling grievances which arise out of specific conditions on the job. Management likewise devotes a great deal of time and energy not only to adjustment of grievances but to elimination of causes of worker dissatisfactions as well. In other words, collective bargaining usually provides a strong incentive for the company to "clean up its backyard and keep it as tidy as possible." The "winning of concessions" by the union in each new contract, moreover, tends to create the impression among workers that they are doing a pretty good job of periodically and systematically "shaking down the boss" for their share of the fruits of economic progress. Every time a wage increase is won through the collective-bargaining process, the worker probably feels more satisfied with collective bargaining and a little happier about living under the private-enterprise system. Although very few workers participate actively in the affairs of their union, they appear to have confidence in the ability of union leaders, acting as their "Philadelphia lawyers," to keep an eye on management and to voice effectively their interests. Thus, the leader of a radical movement who would overthrow or in any way alter this very satisfying and successful method of getting "more" from the employers finds little support among modern rank-and-file workers.

The humanizing influence of collective bargaining on modern capitalism, though perhaps not so obvious, is none the less of profound importance. Many of our outstanding economists have postulated the idea that the optimum allocation of economic resources stems from the mechanistic operation of blind and impersonal forces. They are also likely to refer to labour as a "commodity" or as "another factor of production" in an economic system which works best when each participant uses it as a vending machine. This kind of intellectual rationale, of course, is repugnant to workers who are convinced that labour has values distinguishing it from, and placing it above, other factors of production. A worker is conditioned by his parents, by his teachers, and by all the media of mass communication to believe that he is born free and equal, is endowed with the right to seek redress of grievances wherever they arise, and is heir to an economic system guaranteeing him the right to work and to earn a good living. The emphasis which collective bargaining places on human values, therefore, provides him with a rationale for believing in the existing enterprise system. The very process of establishing wages through bargaining, even if income levels of workers may not be substantially influenced, gives workers a feeling that blind economic forces are being properly tempered by human forces.

The process of collective bargaining also absorbs the energies and interests of many leaders of the working masses who might otherwise direct their energies to the overthrow of the existing economic order. Most students of labour movements would agree, I think, that the more a union leader concentrates on collective bargaining, the more conservative he is likely to become. American labour leaders, almost without exception, have moved from left to right as they have gained experience with, and become absorbed by, the process of negotiating and administering treaties with employers. To the extent that collective bargaining appears to bring results and to command the support of the rank and file, the labour leader devotes more time and energy to it; and, to the extent that he concentrates on bargaining, the chances are that he may make it more successful. This is, of course, one of the reasons why the American labour movement is so job-centred rather than politically oriented.

For all these reasons collective bargaining is an institution which bolsters the existing economic order in our country. It flourishes and survives only in the climate of private enterprise. It both creates the machinery and provides the rationale for endorsement of capitalism by employers, labour leaders, and workers.

Finally, I think that most honest analysts of collective bargaining would agree that, on balance, it has resulted in a reasonable measure of industrial peace. There are strikes, to be sure, and some of them have brought great inconvenience to the public, but it would be difficult indeed to show that strikes have had any appreciable or long-lasting adverse effect on economic growth, economic stability, business prosperity, or levels of investment. In the United States, strike activity has been on the wane since the end of the Second World War. In 1962, for example, the percentage of man-hours lost from strikes in relationship to man-hours worked was 0.16, and it appears that this figure may be declining rather than rising. To some extent, strikes teach the parties how to avoid future strikes. In many industries, there are long periods of industrial peace after a serious strike. If we use a grading system, on the score of industrial peace, collective bargaining should be given a clear pass, even if it is a low one.

Thus, on balance, collective bargaining has had a constructive impact, at least in the United States. It comes out with flying colours in two major areas; it clearly passes as a constructive force in a third; and only in one area, the economic, has it been on the failing side, and even here the failure, if indeed it is one at all, is a marginal one.

The Limitations of Collective Bargaining

Collective bargaining is a limited-purpose institution. It cannot be expected to solve all the problems of modern industrial society. Today's critics of collective bargaining expect it to perform miracles which lie far beyond its legitimate scope. Collective bargaining cannot contribute much to the solution of the admittedly serious problems of chronic unemployment, inadequate economic growth, persistent balance of payments difficulties, underdeveloped systems of education, pre-employment vocational training, or civil rights. It certainly has not helped to stem inflation, nor has it been a bulwark against deflation. Does this constitute a valid criticism of collective bargaining? Certainly not! Why should one expect collective bargaining to solve such problems?

Unions are pressure organizations representing employed workers. They are not vitally concerned, other than for altruistic reasons, with the unemployed, with high school drop-outs seeking work, or with pre-employment education and training. They are not likely to put pressure on employers to hire Negroes or other disadvantaged groups particularly if the jobs of existing union members are jeopardized thereby. The effective pressure for civil rights in the United States came from groups other than organized labour and organized business. Enterprise management, likewise, cannot be expected to take up cudgels for the unemployed or those who are discriminated against in employment. The problems of economic growth, and also to a considerable extent unemployment, are better tackled by increasing aggregate demand. Here appropriate monetary and fiscal policies rather than collective-bargaining procedures must provide the fundamental answers. One should not reasonably expect that these global economic and social problems can be solved by collective bargaining, no matter how "statesmanlike" it may be.

Labour organizations and management groups, of course, express opinions and have legitimate concerns in these broad areas. But they are not prepared, and rightly so, to use pressure based upon the ultimate resort to force in order to achieve objectives in these areas. These areas lie beyond the mainstream of their vital interests which are wages, benefits, job protection, managerial rights, profits, and organizational survival and sovereignty. In a pluralistic society there are other special interest groups in addition to unions and employer organizations, which seek proprietorship over broad issues of national economic and social policy. In this broader arena, organized labour and management play a role in shaping national policy, but they must share the stage with a host of other actors. Management and labour organizations can play constructive roles in the arena, but here their activities lie beyond the scope of collective bargaining.

Collective bargaining obviously has more direct relevance on automation and technological progress. The invention of new devices and processes and the development of the techniques of automation lie beyond the scope of bargaining, but their introduction does not. Union and management bargainers can negotiate the adaptation of the working forces to automation. Yet, it is unreasonable to expect that collective bargaining can prevent the displacement of men by machines, find new jobs for all who are displaced, and provide appropriate training for all those who must acquire new skills. In the modern industrial society, these matters call for much broader consideration than the parties at the collective-bargaining table can provide.

Finally, in modern industrial societies collective bargaining cannot remain free of all intervention by government. It is no longer an exercise by two major protagonists—management and organized labour—with the government serving as referee. Government is quite legitimately a third force at the bargaining table. In the "key bargains" in industries such as steel, automobiles, transportation, and public services government is also a pressure-generating force. The government has exerted pressure, and will continue to use pressure, to induce labour and management to reach accommodations in so-called emergency disputes. It will establish guidelines for appropriate ranges of economic settlements which it feels are vital to the national interest in promoting economic growth and preserving economic stability. Although it is not necessary for government to have a legal right to outlaw strikes and order settlements, it is clear that government must and will exercise its influence and exert strong pressure to make collective-bargaining agreements conform to the broader interests of the public. The entry of government as a silent or even an active participant in bargaining need not impair the constructive consequences of collective bargaining as outlined above. In collective bargaining the parties must respond to the pressures in a "squeeze-box," and these pressures may include those emanating from the public interest and channellized by government.

4

Collective Bargaining and the Challenge of Technological Change

ARNOLD R. WEBER°

WITH THE EXCEPTION of the birth of quintuplets and manned space flights, few activities have been the object of such close scrutiny as collective bargaining. Virtually every government official, economist, and newspaper editor has his own fever chart which describes the present condition of the subject. The slightest rise in temperature elicits anxious concern and a variety of remedies ranging from stiff legislative prescriptions to imported patent medicines. Not content with these judgments, the conference chairman has placed us under a mandate to carry out a wide-ranging assessment of collective bargaining. Because Professor Harbison has accomplished this task so well, and because I agree with much that he said, I have reduced the scope of my discussion to more modest dimensions. Rather than dealing with the broad aspects of collective bargaining, I will focus on the details of a specific set of responses to a particular challenge; that of technological change. Although this approach probably would not satisfy Toynbee it will, I hope, serve the more practical objective of complementing Professor Harbison.

°Graduate School of Business, University of Chicago.

One more disclaimer is in order. That is, for the greater part my comments will apply directly to developments that have taken place in the United States. It's a full-time job keeping up with Mr. Hoffa, let alone Mr. Banks. However, the trends and issues to be identified are also broadly relevant to the Canadian situation. This is not said because of any latent intellectual imperialism. Instead, the similarity of developments in the two countries reflects the fact that, for better or worse, they are linked together by common ties among unions and business enterprises and share many legal and cultural traditions. Indeed, cogent parallels can be made between North American and Western European experiences as well. An appreciation of, and sensitivity to, differences in institutional arrangements should not obscure similarities which arise from economic considerations that cross national boundaries.

THE CHALLENGE TO COLLECTIVE BARGAINING

Observers of the current scene rarely demonstrate sufficient insight to identify periods of momentous change as they occur. However, it seems evident that collective bargaining is presently confronted with the second major challenge of this century. The first challenge arose after the Second World War and reflected the massive gains in trade union membership that had been made in the previous decade. The task of labour-management relations was to develop procedures for the responsible use of power. Major industries were shaken by prolonged strikes which caused considerable concern that the parties lacked the maturity to resolve their differences autonomously. The postwar upheaval proved to be short-lived. Since that time, the incidence of strikes has trended steadily downward, and unions and management alike have demonstrated the ability to develop reasonably constructive relationships. Although the verdict is far from unanimous, there is wide agreement that collective bargaining met the test and has become a permanent feature of the industrial relations systems in the United States and Canada.

The second major challenge to labour-management relations

is different in nature. If the first test involved the capacity of organized labour and its corporate counterparts to create a framework for accommodation, this second, contemporary challenge focuses on the ability of the parties to cope with dramatic alterations in the environment within which they interact. This development has taken place against a backdrop of extensive technological change, popularly identified as "automation." Clearly, automation is to industrial engineering as sex was to psychology. That is, it has kindled the public's interest in a heretofore obscure branch of knowledge while giving rise to fears of dire consequences if the practice is carried too far.

Broadly speaking, automation involves the substitution of machines for human effort and judgment in the implementation and control of production. Although automation in the technical sense has been with us for a long time, the tempo and scope of its application have increased substantially in the last fifteen years. Antiquarians may derive some comfort from tracing automation back to Oliver Evans' flour mill in eighteenth century Delaware, but automation in the modern sense owes more to the petroleum refining industry and the now obsolete Ford engine block plant in Cleveland than to these venerable examples of colonial ingenuity. One index of the pace and extent of the diffusion of technical change is provided by the example of the computer. The first computer to be placed "on the line" in the United States was used by the Bureau of the Census in 1951 to aggregate and analyse the results of the 1950 census. At present, there are over 16,000 known computers in operation in industry and government and the number seems to be growing at an increasing rate.

Automation has had a direct and indirect impact on a wide range of economic, social, and psychological considerations. The literature is replete with commentaries relating automation to everything from education to the incidence of lower-back injuries. While such analyses may be useful and significant, they are of limited relevance to industrial relations developments. When assessing the impact of technological change on collective bargaining, changes in the level and structure of employment opportunities will exercise the most profound influence on the policies of the participants. Although Canadian unions have been more venturesome in political affairs, they appear to have the same bread-and-butter orientation at the bargaining table as their American counterparts. Thus, as technological change has impinged on the labour force, trade union leaders on both sides of the border probably have watched monthly employment reports with the preoccupation of a sea captain eyeing the barometer as his ship enters heavy seas.

In fact, the effect of recent technological change on employment levels cannot be easily determined. As the unit of analysis is expanded from the plant and the individual firm to a particular industry and the economy, it becomes increasingly difficult to isolate the impact of automation from the host of other variables that determine the level of employment. The difficulty of making aggregate estimates of the employment effect of automation becomes more acute when total output and employment are increasing, as they have been for the past several years.

Any ambiguity about the effect of automation on employment opportunities is removed when examining particular plant or office situations. Essentially, the consequences of automation for labour-management relations in the United States and Canada are linked to what happens in the work place. That is, industrial relations in both countries are still highly decentralized and programs to deal with technical change will largely reflect the perspectives of the worker rather than the President's Council of Economic Advisers. Thus it is undeniable that in many specific instances technical change, i.e., automation, has resulted in a net reduction in employment. This consequence has been observed in particular plants in the meat packing, oil refining, electronics, coal, steel, and paper industries. In addition, when the computer enters the office it has shown the same dispassionate efficiency in sorting out people as it demonstrates in dealing with punched cards. The magnitude of the reduction varies, of course, with the extent of the change and other variables. In some cases, however, the decline in employment has exceeded 50 per cent.

Second, automation has been a powerful force contributing to changes in the structure of the labour force. Recent technological advances have dealt the heaviest blows to semi-skilled operatives and industrial labourers—those groups that have long been the exemplification of blue-collar virtue. At the same time, automation has contributed to gains in the number of professional and technical workers, mechanics, repairmen and other occupational groups concerned with the development and maintenance of complex productive equipment. In aggregate, automation has reinforced other trends in the economy which have undermined the dominance of blue-collar workers. Despite the recent "comeback" of the blue-collar worker it is significant to note that the number of semi-skilled operatives has only regained the level attained at the peak of the last boom in 1956, while industrial production increased by 32 percent between 1956 and 1964.

Further evidence of these shifts in the structure of the labour force is provided by the various case studies of the impact of automation. In almost every situation, jobs have been most drastically eliminated at the lower rungs of the occupational ladder. In the typical industrial plant this means the abolition of jobs for materials-handling and machine operatives. In the office, the computer is making the bookkeeper and file clerk as obsolete as the goose quill. One study of the introduction of the computer into an Internal Revenue Service district office revealed that as many as 80 per cent of the bookkeepers' jobs were eliminated.

Although the chain of causation becomes more indirect, a third consequence of automation for employment warrants some attention here. When a firm introduces a major technical change it is likely to make other basic economic adjustments, particularly those relating to the geographical location of production facilities. In the meat packing industry, for example, shifts in population and changes in the marketing of livestock have undermined the economic attractions of traditional centres of production such as Chicago and Kansas City. Thus, when advanced technology is introduced it probably will be in a new plant located in an area that meets a broad range of economic requirements. Similar developments have taken place in the automobile, paper, and textile industries. Many of the depressed areas in the United States attest to the effect of this geographical redistribution of employment opportunities.

While the employment effects of current technological change press on the central ganglia of union and management officials, it is important to note that automation also impinges on other major collective-bargaining issues. Under the conditions posed by new technology, adjustments may be required in existing seniority systems. Established methods of wage payment often come under close examination. And work schedules may be modified because of changes in the nature of the production process.

Each of these issues merit detailed investigation. However, beyond these specific points of controversy, there is the broader question of the impact of technological change on the character of collective bargaining itself. The discussion on this larger issue will focus on three areas; power relationships and bargaining tactics, bargaining procedures, and the substantive methods for dealing with technological change through collective bargaining. It is probably superfluous but none-the-less necessary to note that collective-bargaining developments in the United States and Canada have consistently confounded the best guesses of generations of experts.

POWER RELATIONSHIPS AND BARGAINING TACTICS

Power, as many observers have noted, is a basic component of collective bargaining. On balance, it appears that current technological change has strengthened management's hand at the bargaining table. First, there is a loose proportional relationship between union membership and union power. To the extent that automation dampens union growth it will limit the economic pressure that can be brought to bear on the employer. In fact, union membership gains have lagged in both countries so that labour organizations command the allegiance of a smaller proportion of the labour force than they did fifteen years ago.

Many factors, of course, lie behind the inability of trade

unions to broaden their membership base. These include changes in public policy, worker attitudes towards unionism, and increased management sophistication in dealing with personnel problems. However, these factors have been reinforced by technical changes that are eroding the relative importance of traditional centres of union strength and promoting growth in those sectors which historically have been the most difficult to organize. The successful organizing drives of the 1930's were largely built upon the ability of union leaders to organize the militant discontents of the unskilled and semi-skilled workers in the extractive and mass producing industries. It is precisely these occupational categories which are bearing the brunt of displacement associated with automation. Despite strenuous efforts and the recent "comeback of the blue-collar worker," unions like the Automobile Workers, the Steel Workers, and the Meat Packing Workers have never regained the heights they reached in 1953–4. Similarly, membership in the former behemoth of the labour movement, the United Mine Workers, probably has declined by more than 50 per cent since the end of the Second World War. Sustained by an aging membership which fought the union's battles more than two decades ago, the conventions of the UMW are reminiscent of the commemorative encampments of the Grand Army of the Republic at the turn of the century.

If any major breakthroughs are made by the trade union movement, they will have to come in the expanding white-collar sector. One careful study indicates that in the United States only 2.5 million white-collar workers, or approximately 5 per cent of the total white-collar sector of the labour force, are currently union members. As might be expected, union leaders at the highest echelon have been giving concentrated attention to this problem. Thus far, their efforts have been greeted with only limited success and it does not appear that the extension of office automation will create a more propitious climate for white-collar unionism. Although the introduction of the computer and associated hardware into the office invariably will have a disruptive effect on the work force, managers today are forewarned and have been armed with a battery of personnel procedures to avert unionization during the changeover to the new technology. Any inroads that unions make in the office will be hard fought and gained over a long period of time. The Metropolitan Insurance Company is unlikely to capitulate *in toto* as United States Steel did thirty years ago.

Second, union power may be diminished by the nature of the new technology. Automation, by definition, implies greater automaticity in the operation of the production process. Therefore, when a trade union initiates a strike, the effectiveness of this sanction may be reduced by the company's ability to operate using supervisors and other managerial personnel. For example, it is increasingly difficult to mount a successful strike in the telephone, gas and electric utility, chemical, and oil refining industries. In the oil industry, the Oil, Chemical, and Atomic Workers Union has fought several bitter battles with companies in the last five years. In each case, management maintained production at a satisfactory level through the use of management personnel. A dramatic manifestation of management's ability to diminish union power occurred during the strike at the Shell refinery in Houston, Texas. In that case, the Refinery continued to operate at high levels of capacity while the struggle dragged on for a year. Similarly, during a twenty-eight-day strike at the Brooklyn Gas Company there was not a single cold pot of chicken soup in Brooklyn as the firm continued operations. This immunity to the union's economic power has not been attained in industries like steel, autos, construction, and transportation. It is significant, however, that the strike has been neutralized in several important sectors of the economy.

Although automation may, in the long run, reduce trade union's striking power, paradoxically, those strikes that do occur in the next few years are likely to be long and perhaps bitter. On the one hand, many of the issues arising within a context of automation are of extreme importance to both parties: the union seeks to preserve employment opportunities for its members, while management sees the new technology as a broom to sweep clean many of the inefficient practices that have accumulated over the past twenty years. The problem of achieving an accommodation is frequently accentuated by the technical complexity of the controversies. Unlike a strike over wages, the issues are not easily compromised by agreeing on some manifest middle position.

On the other hand, union leaders are doubtless aware that the new technology is blunting the effectiveness of the strike weapon. Therefore, they may be moved to use their power before it is undermined by technical change. In this manner, the union may still be able to command respect at the bargaining table because every time management squirms in indignation at the union's demands it can feel the welts inflicted in previous rounds. Some of this long-run strategy has probably entered into the prolonged tests of power that recently have taken place in the newspaper industry. The industry is presently in a period of revolutionary change and it seems likely that the unions' ability to deal with an adamant employer through direct confrontation of power will be significantly reduced in the future.

In addition to wielding its remaining spears with increased vigour there is also some indication that American unions are consolidating their forces so that they may function more effectively in the new technological and market environment. Union mergers, in contrast to corporate marriages, are usually defensive in -nature. Moreover, the tendency toward consolidation is accentuated by the fact that automation is blurring traditional jurisdictional lines. Mergers involving the Chemical and Oil Workers, the Lithographers and Photoengravers, and two paper workers' unions are cases in point. Meanwhile, sporadic negotiations have been carried out among other printing trades groups and the railroad brotherhoods. It is conjectural whether such consolidations will be sufficiently far-reaching to have significant effect on power relationships in collective bargaining. In many instances, internal political factors have presented insuperable barriers to merger. However, the sophisticated union leader is on notice that the Wagner Act and provincial statutes did not exempt them from the Darwinian laws of survival.

CHANGING BARGAINING PROCEDURES

The din of the past and prospective battles should not divert attention from the constructive activities that have taken place at the bargaining table. In an effort to arrive at solutions to the problems associated with technological change, unions and management have developed a major innovation in collective-bargaining procedures—the joint study committee. Such committees have been established in a wide variety of industries which encompass the dominant collective-bargaining relationships in the United States, including steel, automobile, meat packing, newspaper, publishing, longshoring, glass, and agricultural implements. The demand for the formation of these committees was so great at one point that the management of one automobile supply firm with annual sales of $300 million dollars ruefully reported that the UAW had refused its request for a joint study group because the company was too small to justify the use of scarce union staff resources.

In many cases the study committees have not been formed explicitly to deal with the issues arising from automation. It is not coincidental, however, that this innovation has been most widely adopted in those situations in which the scope and pace of change have posed severe threats to the stability of union-management relationships. In addition items dealing with the dislocation stemming from the introduction of new technology frequently have been given top positions on the committee's agendas. The distinguishing characteristic of the joint study committee is the intensive analysis of a limited number of problems by union and management representatives during the term of the collective-bargaining agreement. In some cases, the committee is expanded to include neutral third parties. This apparently innocuous instrument can, and has had, a profound effect upon the bargaining process, especially when vital interests are at stake.

First, the joint study committee often has been a vehicle for informal advance notice of technological change well before the change takes place. In the absence of the committee such notification usually would be limited to the narrow requirements of the contract. Moreover, the highly charged atmosphere during negotiations over the contract terms is hardly the appropriate time for the sober consideration of the company's plans.

Second, the joint study committee has permitted the parties to engage in bilateral fact-finding concerning the probable consequences of technological change and the feasibility of alternative remedial programs. The topics studied have ranged from the protection of future employment in the meat packing industry to possible measures of productivity in longshoring and the cost of an extended vacation plan for the employees of the basic steel producers. Such bilateral fact-finding does not constitute a shortcut to harmonious relationships, but it does help to provide a neutral framework within which controversies based on conflicting interests may be resolved.

Third, the study committee has helped to free the bargaining process from the political pressures and rigid adversary roles that often characterize contract negotiations. In most cases, the ground rules for the committee deliberations specify that the parties can make statements without fear of retribution or subsequent accusations of inconsistency. In addition, the discussions usually are carried out on a confidential basis so that a free exchange of ideas and information can take place without exciting premature responses from the committee members' constituents. The fact that the study groups carry out their activities long before contract termination periods also helps to maintain a low-key atmosphere and spirit of flexibility.

Fourth, the joint study committee approach has encouraged a certain degree of experimentation in the development of programs to cope with new economic conditions. The Armour Automation Fund Committee introduced important modifications in the operation of an interplant transfer program with the understanding that the changes would not be binding if they did not work to the satisfaction of the parties. A similar escape clause was linked to a formula that was developed by the Human Relations Committee in the steel industry for dealing with subcontracting. In a more dramatic case, the Long Range Sharing Plan devised by the study committee in Kaiser Steel also permits either party to withdraw from the program after the appropriate period of notice. With the knowledge that all mistakes are not irreversible, unions and managements may be expected to demonstrate a greater venturesomeness in collective bargaining.

The achievements of the joint study committees have been notable in several situations. The effort to find a measure for productivity in longshoring operations resulted eventually in the pathbreaking Modernization and Mechanization Agreement on the Pacific Coast. The Armour Automation Fund Committee has carried out a program for the interplant transfer and retraining of workers displaced by the shutdown of obsolete plants. And the Human Relations Committee did much of the spade work for a variety of measures aimed at enhancing the steelworkers' job security.

The joint study committee approach has not been without its shortcomings or failures. In some instances its adoption seemed to represent a vacuous faddism in industrial relations or a tactic to postpone the consideration of hard problems. Thus the committees established in the automobile industry appear to have had little effect on the course of collective bargaining to date. Nor is there any indication that a study committee has melted the freeze in union-management relations in the New York City newspaper industry. In other cases, the confidential aspects of committee deliberations incurred the suspicions of the rank and file and became a political issue within the union. This was an important factor leading to the demise of the Human Relations Committee in the steel industry. To add to this chorus, the leadership of the Packinghouse Workers has attacked the Automation Fund Committee as a "publicity gimmick" but significantly did not force a dissolution of the group at the last contract negotiations.

It is also clear that the study committees will not, or cannot, supplant the essential power aspects of the collective-bargaining process. Instead, they serve the cause of rationality primarily by neutralizing potential controversies over factual questions and by providing some assurance that power will not be exercised over trivial matters. Where the issues are extremely complicated, as in dealing with technological change, these gains may be well worth the price.

PROGRAMS FOR ADJUSTMENT

Despite the signs of impatience and antagonism on both sides, the parties generally have responded with restraint and imagination to the problems posed by automation. Out of a sense of realism or responsibility, few unions have adopted a posture of outright resistance to technological change. Management also has shown a disposition to recognize problems of transition that it studiously ignored in the past. And the use of new procedures has contributed to the variety of measures adopted to deal with the consequences of automation. From this range of experience, three general approaches may be identified; the buy-out, gains-sharing, and manpower management.

The buy-out approach generally involves an attempt to indemnify the worker for economic losses imposed by technical change. The problem of adjustment is then one of arriving at some acceptable formula for estimating the costs to the individual and making restitution as the "property rights" in his job are liquidated. In most cases, these formulae lay no claim to precision. Instead, they are broadly related to previous earnings levels and length of service.

The most widely used form of indemnification for loss of employment is severance pay. Here, a lump sum payment is made to the employee when his job is permanently terminated because of automation or associated economic adjustment. Severance pay provisions are found in many labour-management agreements today and are generally considered a starting point for subsequent attempts to deal with the problems of technological change. In other instances, extended Supplemental Unemployment Benefits augment or replace the concept of severance pay. However, the difference between the two is largely formal in the sense that SUB involves a flow of income over time rather than a single lump-sum payment.

The buy-out has reached its highest refinement in the transportation industries. On the railroads, the Washington Job Protection Agreement, negotiated in 1936 to deal with displacement arising from the merger of two or more carriers, provides the basic framework for the indemnification of employees affected by technological change. Under this approach, workers who are displaced or who are "made worse off" as a consequence of the new conditions are provided with compensatory income payments over a specfied period of time, usually five years. This formula has been incorporated in various agreements negotiated between the Brotherhood of Railway Clerks and different carriers to deal with the intro- duction of electronic data processing systems in offices. It also was a key concept in the arbitration decision that ended the passion play arising from the dispute over the deisel fireman in the United States. As evidence of the continuous flow of ideas and experience across the border, a similar formula, albeit more generous, was an important ingredient in the recom- mendations of the Kellock Commission which paved the way for the earlier resolution of the fireman issue in Canada in 1959.

The historic agreement between the Pacific Maritime Association and the International Longshoremen and Ware- housemen's Union also represents an advanced adaptation of the buy-out formula. In this case, the employers agreed to pay $27.5 million into a special fund over a period of five years. The proceeds of this fund are used to finance wage guarantees and special retirement benefits. Each fully registered long- shoreman has a proprietary claim to $7,920 which he may exercise in one form or another.

The buy-out has several advantages to recommend it to both management and unions. As part of the bargain, management is generally given considerable latitude in the introduction of technical change and, once it has translated its "moral respon- sibility" into financial terms, it can go about the task of increas- ing efficiency with few restraints. The freedom to modify existing work rules was a major incentive in the West Coast maritime case. The Union, in turn, sees the indemnification payments as a factor retarding the pace at which technical change may be introduced. That is, where management has to make sizable cash payments in the form of earnings, guaran- tees, or severance pay to its employees, the calculation of costs and returns may temporarily tip the balance in favour of the *status quo*. In addition, once the lump sum payments are made to the employees they serve as "social shock absorbers" to tide the displaced employee over the period of transition in the labour market at large.

Gain-sharing, the second approach to the problems of automation, also attempts to translate the consequences of technical change into monetary terms. Management is again afforded wide discretion in introducing change while some formula is contrived for distributing the gains from productivity among employees. However, whereas the buy-out generally is directed at those who are displaced, the gain-sharing approach manifests greater solicitude to those who continue to work.

The classic example of the gain-sharing approach to technological change is provided by the bituminous coal industry. In this case, John L. Lewis long ago made a basic policy decision that it would be more desirable to have fewer coal miners working at high wages than to have many coal miners employed at what he considered marginal wages. Accordingly, the UMW adopted an active policy of encouraging the introduction of labour-saving devices into coal mining operations. The consequences of this policy have been drastic indeed. Unionized coal miners, when they work, are among the highest paid manual workers outside of the building trades in the United States today. At the same time, however, employment in the bituminous coal industry has declined from approximately 450,000 in 1946 to roughly the equivalent of 110,000 full-time employees in 1965. The gains from advancing technology have been shared with the UMW, but their distribution has been limited to a relatively small group.

The Long Range Sharing Plan adopted by the Kaiser Steel Company and the United Steel Workers of America, provides another example of the gain-sharing approach. Here, a complicated formula has been established for passing on to the members of the work force the savings attributable to improved method and technology. The implicit acceptance of gain-sharing as a framework for dealing with technological change may also be noted in many sectors of the building construction industry. In the New York City electrical construction industry, for example, the negotiation of a five-hour day-$5.50 per hour bulwark against the employment effects of technological change was accompanied by several concessions to management that would promote the application of new methods.

It is obvious that the gain-sharing approach, by itself, has limited promise in facilitating adjustments to technological change. That is, it tends to distribute income only among a favoured few. For this reason, it is normally used in company and industry situations where management is confronted with intense competition and where total employment opportunities do not decline too sharply. When there are major reductions in the number of jobs available, extreme pressures are likely to develop within the union because of the discrepancy in the economic welfare of the members. This situation has developed in the coal industry where a rash of wildcat strikes has underscored the discontent of the rank and file with the absence of comprehensive provisions for job security.

The manpower planning approach generally rejects the economic maxim that every man has his price. Instead, it emphasizes the need for distributing employment opportunities as widely as possible among union members. In some cases, manpower planning may also involve efforts to promote the occupational mobility of displaced workers in the external labour market once displacement has been carried out. Within the firm, detailed studies are made to determine the level and structure of employment opportunities in the immediate future and to establish criteria for allocating these opportunities among workers with different priorities.

Historically, the manpower planning approach may be traced back to traditional forms of work-sharing. But recent programs have gone beyond this simple formula. First, attrition has been widely used to reduce the level of employment while minimizing actual displacement. Thus, workers are not replaced as they die, resign, or retire. In addition, systematic efforts have been made to induce attrition by the negotiation of generous early retirement plans. Second, collective-bargaining agreements in the auto, steel, meat packing, and glass industries, among others, have established interplant transfer plans so that workers who are displaced by technical change or plant shutdowns in one location may exercise a claim to employment opportunities opening up in other installations. Third, active steps have been taken to retrain workers for new jobs in the firm or labour market at large. Fourth, greater emphasis is being placed on sharing the gains of productivity in the form of compensated leisure rather than increased monetary income. In this respect, there has been both augmentation of conventional vacation plans and a willingness to experiment with new programs. The so-called industrial sabbatical negotiated in the steel industry affords high-seniority workers extended vacations of up to thirteen weeks every five years. A novel variant of this approach developed by the Packinghouse workers and the American Sugar Refining Company limits these extended vacations to workers who are over fifty-five years of age. This modification opens up greater employment opportunities for the younger workers while ostensibly preparing the older employees for the delights of the golden years.

None of the three approaches devised by collective bargaining for handling the problems of automation leads to an economic promised land. The buy-out primarily serves to provide the deceased with a decent burial. There is no guarantee that they will be able to adjust to a new labour market environment without considerable deprivation. Gain-sharing tends to promote the interests of the residual job holders. And manpower planning can largely facilitate distribution of available employment opportunities.

In practice, a combination of approaches has been employed in handling the consequence of technological change in particular collective-bargaining situations, although there are significant differences in emphasis from case to case. Moreover, once some provision is made for indemnification, there is a pronounced tendency for the parties to move toward what has been called manpower management. In many ways, this approach puts the greatest burdens on unions and management in collective bargaining because it continually requires the development of new programs and administrative procedures to fit the specific circumstances of a particular plant or office situation. But it also offers the brightest prospects for minimizing the economic and social costs of a difficult period of transition.

CONCLUSION

In the last year, the public and professional concern over the consequences of technological change has perceptibly subsided. This shift in attitudes reflects several factors. Undoubtedly, the initial fears regarding automation were exaggerated. In addition, fiscal policies have blunted the cutting edge of unemployment. Beyond these factors it is clear, however, that collective bargaining has made a major contribution to the process of adjustment. It has helped to create a greater awareness of the specific dimensions of the problem where casual indifference or empty generalizations might have prevailed. It has substituted orderly procedures for improvisation. It has sought some acceptable basis for distributing the costs and benefits of the new technology among those who are directly affected. And it generally has carried out these functions without the promiscuous exercise of power.

As part of a decentralized system of decision-making, the contributions made by collective bargaining inevitably are limited by the scope of the units under the parties' control. Within this constraint, however, collective bargaining has responded to the challenge of technological change with more vitality than resignation. Despite the forebodings of its friends and the hopes of its enemies, collective bargaining will continue to play an important role in mediating the claims of competing economic groups.

5

Challenge and Response in the Law of Labour Relations

HARRY W. ARTHURS*

CHALLENGE AND RESPONSE in the law are by no means confined to the area of labour relations. In many areas of law, which touch upon controversial social questions, there is a continual and a healthy tension between law and life. Law, after all, is a technique for preserving order and stability in society, for substituting calm and reasoned judgment for passion and violent pursuit of self-interest. Necessarily, however, the order and stability which law represents take the form of a prevailing social consensus. Thus, before the law can change, it is necessary for society's thinking to change. Inevitably, then, there is a cultural lag between legal and social values. This lag is accentuated by our few, slow, and clumsy techniques for law reform. As someone has put it, the problem is that judges will not and legislators cannot.

The common law, at best, is laboriously built, case upon case, over a period of years. Thus, it is extremely unlikely that the development of a common law doctrine will be much altered once its foundations are laid. Such shifts as do take place are likely to be marginal, and often surreptitious. Moreover, the common law judge can only speak when a litigant brings a case to him. Thus, even if the courts were receptive to change,

*Osgoode Hall Law School.

it might be years before the appropriate occasion arose,
especially since the facts of a particular case are crucial in
determining its outcome. I suspect that you will agree the
common law is likely to respond to social challenges with
something less than haste. I say nothing of the propriety or
otherwise of judges deciding fundamental, yet delicate, issues
of public policy.

More and more, however, we have turned to the legislatures
to solve labour problems. Yet, here again, the law does not
automatically change its course to adapt to new challenges.
Typically, labour relations legislation is the product of vigorous
and belligerent lobbying by each side for a new law with which
to club the other into submission. It is extremely unlikely that
the loser in this legislative donnybrook will accept the new law
in good grace, and will make it work well. It must be emphasized, moreover, that the relationship between life and law,
between social challenge and legal response, is one of reci-
procity. Just as the law changes slowly to produce new solutions for the industrial relations community, so too the law's
impact upon that community produces new problems which in
turn demand their own solution.

Yet, the great challenges are external to the law and are
produced by the dynamics of industrial relations. Set against
the background of a rather rigid and unresponsive legal
system, these seem swifter and more urgent. Consider some of
the recent developments in the world of industrial relations,
and the challenges they must pose to the legal system. Trite
indeed it is to observe that our world is ever more rapidly
changing in its technology, in its complexity and interdepen-
dence. What is less frequently observed is a rapid and profound revolution of our expectations. In international relations,
it is no doubt the very magnitude of potential conflict which
has produced an earnest, and occasionally successful, search
for new techniques of peace keeping. Not all of these techniques seek to end conflict as it erupts. The vast proliferation
of international agencies of aid and collaboration is intended
to strike at the very roots of discontent. By assisting the "have-
not" countries, the "haves" hope to preserve the peace, while
gaining good-will. A less cynical interpretation of events might

be that we are finally recognizing our international moral responsibilities. But whether their motives are selfish or noble, we have come to expect more of nations. So, too, with the world of industrial relations. In an increasingly complex economy, caught up in a process of technological change, we are in the midst of a revolution of expectations. Yesterday we were prepared to contemplate strikes as an inevitable adjunct of collective bargaining. Tomorrow, we may no longer let the parties make war. Indeed, even today we are no longer content that industrial strife should be speedily ended. We have begun to anticipate strife, and to eradicate its causes. We have, I feel, begun to introduce a new element of morality into our judgment of how labour and management should behave.

Is our law attuned to these new developments? I suggest not. Technology changes quickly, yet the parties often freeze their relationships in a collective agreement binding for two or three years and cannot legally sign an agreement for less than one. Our problems are constantly more complex, yet our legislative policy is designed to encourage collective bargaining only on the basic issues of wages and working conditions. Our social and economic units are increasingly interdependent, yet our constitution fragments nation-wide bargaining into provincial patterns, and our statutes put a premium on the single-employer bargaining unit. And finally, our law of labour relations embodies the low expectations, the old morality, of the 1930's and '40's. No more is demanded than a minimal and murky statutory duty to "bargain in good faith" and adherence to a judicially drafted set of Marquis of Queensberry rules for industrial warfare.

I think that I have already said enough to indicate that the challenge for men of law is to avoid the collision of irresistible social forces and immoveable legal objects.

I

Let me look first at the law as an immoveable object rigid in both procedure and substance. Two basic, but often clashing, values in the law are speed and fairness. Of course, in industrial relations, time is always of the essence. A union awaiting certification may see its support ebb away over a period of weeks or months; an employer threatened with picket line pressure may lose thousands of dollars in a single day; the relative bargaining strength of the parties may be greatly altered if negotiations are protracted into or beyond peak production periods. Yet, there is always the danger that in attempting to move with the rapid pace of events, legal procedures may be less than fair. Three quite different examples come to mind.

Crucial to understanding the current controversy over the use of the labour injunction is realization of the fact that it involves these legitimate but competing values—speed and fairness. The employer's interest is in speed: for him time is money. The union, accused of wrongdoing, takes its stand on the issue of fairness: for it, time is the opportunity to prepare and present a defence. To some extent, the unions' position was vindicated when we virtually abolished the *ex parte* injunction in 1960. The legislature apparently decided that confrontation of one's accuser, a basic principle of our legal procedure, was more deserving of protection than speedy protection of an employer's economic interests. This statement is, however, subject to important qualifications. First, violence, destruction of property and disruption of a public service are all enjoinable without notice. These are, no doubt, reasonable exceptions. Second, only in "labour disputes" is the use of the *ex parte* injunction restricted. By a process of judicial interpretation, the term "labour dispute" has been confined to situations where there is a proximate employer-employee relationship. Thus, secondary picketing, organizational and recognition picketing, and other common union tactics, lie beyond the protection of a full hearing. Third, even in cases where notice is given to the offending union, it is frequently a practical impossibility for the union to avail itself of its theoretical privilege to file affidavit material, and to cross-examine the employer's witnesses. Thus, the injunction may be decided on the basis solely of material filed by the plaintiff employer. Fourth, injunction matters are heard in weekly court, where often a list of thirty or forty cases threatens to engulf the most dedicated judge; the time available for a full canvass of the relevant facts and law may be severely limited. Finally, restrictions upon the right of appeal from interlocutory injunction orders mean that the jurisprudence developed by the trial courts has never been thoroughly rationalized by appellate review, at least in Ontario. All of these facts give to labour injunction proceedings an air of unseemly haste. Yet the challenge is clear: if there is wrongful picketing being conducted, with severe financial losses being inflicted upon the employer, is he not entitled to speedy relief?

Other jurisdictions have grappled with this problem, and have not always resolved it satisfactorily. In England, for example, judicial regulation of industrial disputes was all but ended by the Trade Disputes Act of 1906, which immunized unions from most of the causes of action upon which injunctions might be based. Whether recent developments in the English law will lead to a resurrection of the labour injunction in the country of its birth, remains to be seen. In the United States, labour board orders, enforceable in the courts, have displaced the injunction as we know it. Indeed, since 1932 the federal courts of the United States have been explicitly forbidden to issue labour injunctions in all but the most extreme circumstances, and after compliance with carefully stipulated procedural safeguards. Some say that the Labour Board relief is too slow. But is it necessarily beyond the ingenuity of lawyers to strike a reasonable balance between the demands of fairness and those of speed? I think not. But it will not be done by slogan-mongering or academic rumination. We need a thorough statistical analysis of present practices and their consequences. Only with this background of factual information can we lift the search for better techniques above the parochial demands of the parties for arrangements which will most favour their respective positions.

Another interesting procedural problem relates to the introduction of notorious facts into the record in labour litigation. A well-established doctrine of evidence, called "judicial notice," permits the judge to take account of notorious facts to supplement the evidence on the record. The problem is, of course, what facts are notorious? For example, in *Smith Bros.* v. *Jones*, Mr. Justice McLennan took judicial notice of the fact that "the development of the Trade Union movement has reached the point where workers will not cross the picket line to go to work."[1] In *Hersees of Woodstock* v. *Goldstein*, Mr. Justice Aylesworth was prepared, ". . . to take judicial notice that the rule [of respect for the picket line] affects as well, many other members of the public who are not employees . . . particularly where, as at the case at bar, there is a widespread organization of labour. . . ."[2]

Finally, in *Heather Hill Appliances* v. *McCormick*, Mr. Justice Stewart judicially noted that, ". . . a high percentage of unions are dominated by persons from another State whose basic concepts of law, order, good conduct and labour relations are not necessarily ours, but whose control seems to be absolute."[3] His judgment is replete with a variety of amusing and fanciful similes which involve judicial notice as well: management "a long time ago" is characterized as an "unregenerate Scrooge"; a picket line is analogized to "an electric fence" which is said to likewise seem "harmless enough"; and unionists are characterized as "true believers" who will refuse to cross picket lines as "a matter of faith and morals and an obligation of conscience." I merely quote these few illustrations to demonstrate that the courts do not hesitate to supply social data where they think it necessary, by means of judicial notice, even as to such critical matters as the impact of a particular picket line upon a particular employer. I do not necessarily criticize them for doing so, although I confess to serious admiration that men so remote from industrial conflict should be so steeped in its folklore.

On the other hand, the Labour Board, which is presumably staffed by experts in the field of industrial relations, has occasionally been chastised for engaging in a similar practice of officially noting notorious facts of industrial life. Thus, in

---

[1][1955] 4 D.L.R. 254 at p. 264.
[2][1963] 2 O.R. 81 at p. 85 (C.A.).
[3](1965) CCH LLR Para. 14,083 (Ont. H.C.). An appeal to the Court of Appeal, as yet unreported, has been discussed.

the *Tange Company* case,[4] the Ontario Labour Relations Board was held to have legally misconducted itself by reason of taking official notice of its own earlier finding that the Christian Labour Association discriminated on religious grounds against prospective non-Christian members, and was thus ineligible for certification. The case is important, because it demonstrates again the ever-present risk of conflict between speed and fairness. After all, the Christian Labour Association had allegedly changed its policies in the interval and thus could insist on being judged on its present, not its past, practices. Its right to do so is hardly answered by the plea that were the Board obliged to redetermine the status of a union each time it appeared in proceedings, it surely could not function. To be sure, the Board does not always choose speed over fairness. It often seeks full information, and invites the widest range of views, both from the parties and from those who might be affected by the precedent impact of decisions. An example of this is the Board's practice of receiving submissions from local employers and unions before defining geographic areas in construction industry certification cases. This is a sensible, praiseworthy and thoroughly non-judicial procedure. The lawyer's task, sometimes well performed by the Board and sometimes not, is to devise procedures which will allow it to employ its expertise without denying to the parties an opportunity to make a full and effective presentation of their position.

Another illustration of the need of lawyers and legal institutions to develop procedural flexibility is the issue of time limits. The Labour Board Rules, for example, require compliance with a variety of time limits as a condition of contesting certification of a trade union. Similarly, collective agreements customarily specify time limits within which grievances must be filed and processed at succeeding steps. It is natural for law-trained personnel to put great stock in time limits: after all, court litigation is likewise riddled with them. However, proceedings before the Labour Board or arbitration boards are

[4](1961) CCH LLR Para. 16,225 (O.L.R.B.), quashed on certiorari, *sub* nom. *R.* v. *O.L.R.B.*, *ex parte Trenton Construction Workers*, [1963] 2 O.R. 376.

frequently initiated, and often conducted throughout, by laymen; employees are key figures. Yet few laymen and even
fewer employees have any knowledge of even the rudiments of
the collective agreement or the Labour Relations Act, let alone
a sophisticated awareness of the risks of being out of time.
Surely, the challenge here is to develop legal rules to distinguish between those breaches of time limits which have a
discernibly disruptive effect on the conduct of proceedings,
and those which are without prejudice to anyone. Can the law,
then, meet this challenge of flexibility and informality in industrial relations when contrary modes of thought and habits of
business are deeply ingrained as a result of experience in other
kinds of proceedings?

I would like to turn next to the inhibiting effect of precedent
upon the law's response to challenges both internal and external. Lower courts are generally bound by the past decisions of
higher courts. But because higher courts are involved so seldom
in labour relations litigation, most of the governing authority
which controls the day-to-day disposition of cases is remote
both in time and in outlook from modern labour relations. The
leading tort cases in the field, at least until recently, have been
the classic English trilogy, *Allen* v. *Flood*,[5] *Quinn* v. *Leathem*,[6]
Mogul Steamship v. *McGregor*.[7] These cases, decided by the
House of Lords at the turn of the century, are based upon a
suspicion of concerted labour activity. This suspicion runs
directly counter to the assumption in our modern statutes that
collective bargaining is an acceptable way of life. Moreover,
within a few years of being pronounced, the trilogy was
repudiated by the enactment of the 1906 Trade Disputes Act.
It is true, of course, that the recent decisions of the House of
Lords in *Rookes* v. *Barnard*[8] and *Stratford* v. *Lindley*[9] may
have "driven a coach and four" through the 1906 legislation.[9A]
Yet for fifty years or more, the English caselaw, like the

[5][1898] A.C. 1.
[6][1901] A.C. 495.
[7][1892] A.C. 25.
[8][1964] 1 All E.R. 367 (H.L.)
[9][1964] 3 All E.R. 102 (H.L.).
[9A]The impact of these decisions was almost completely nullified by the
Trade Disputes Act, 1965.

English legislation, was marked by judicial reluctance, wise or otherwise, to intervene in industrial disputes. Indeed, even had the English judges been more active, only by coincidence would their decisions have paralleled the labour policy marked out by our legislatures. The inevitable task of meshing common law tort doctrines of yesteryear with the latest legislation has been undertaken with varying degrees of success by our courts.

Most defensible is a line of cases which appears to measure the common law legality of picketing by its impact upon the statutory scheme of industrial relations. Thus, in *Smith Bros.* v. *Jones*[10] and in *Gagnon* v. *Foundation Maritime*,[11] picketing to secure recognition was proscribed because the statute provided a peaceful and lawful procedure by which unions might gain recognition. The certification machinery was intended to remove recognition as a cause of industrial strife and these cases promote the same objective. Likewise in the *Therien*[12] case, failure to resort to the grievance machinery to adjust a dispute over the interpretation of a collective agreement was held to be tortious, because it contravened the statutory policy in favour of arbitration. Again, in the *Nipissing Hotel* case,[13] a union was held liable for asserting economic pressure during negotiations, before exhaustion of the conciliation machinery. Such pressure was held to be wrongful because it subtracted from the union's statutory duty to "bargain in good faith." While one may quibble, on the facts of any of these cases, with its outcome, and with the language in which the decision was couched, I do feel that they represent a useful attempt to integrate statutory policy into the common law.

On the other hand, there are certainly many cases in which the courts have acted totally without reference to statutory guidelines. I feel that the most significant failure of the courts has been in the area of secondary picketing. Here, it seems to me, they have given way to the temptation to make judicial policy out of whole cloth, rather than to merely stitch up the open seams in a well-measured legislative purpose. In Ontario,

[10][1955] 4 D.L.R. 254 (Ont. H.C.).
[11][1961] S.C.R. 435.
[12][1960] S.C.R. 265.
[13](1963) 38 D.L.R. 2d 675 (Ont. H.C.).

as in many other provinces, the Labour Relations Act does not regulate picketing. The only provision touching upon picketing at all is section 57 which forbids the doing of any act which as a reasonable and probable consequence is likely to cause an unlawful strike. A review of the legislative history of this provision quite clearly indicates that it was an extremely limited incursion into the field of picketing generally, and secondary pressures in particular. Indeed, it is further limited by the proviso that it has no application to acts done during the course of a lawful strike. Yet, notwithstanding the refusal of the Ontario legislature to outlaw secondary picketing, as recommended in 1958 by its Select Committee on Labour Relations, our Court of Appeal has done just that. This precedent was followed in a recent Ontario case which forbids so-called secondary picketing by a union, lawfully on strike, at a construction site shared with several other unions. While the non-picketing unions, by tradition, respect the picket line and thus themselves perhaps engage in an unlawful work stoppage, the saving provision of section 57 is clearly intended to ensure that liability falls upon those who stop work unlawfully, and not upon the picketers. But much more significant than the failure to appreciate the rather obscure legislative policy towards picketing is the continued and flourishing development of a body of tort doctrine totally without regard to legislative policies. The case I have referred to effectively prohibits all picketing in the construction industry.

The problem, put shortly, is that the courts have not learned the language of contemporary industrial relations. In this day and age to echo precedent, to talk of inducing breach of contract, of conspiracy to injure, of nuisance, and of other choice items in the judicial "vocabulary of vituperation," is to demonstrate a total lack of understanding of the union tactics against which these doctrines are mobilized. Of course, some of these union tactics are objectionable; some are not. All too often there is simply no investigation of their validity. If the tactic falls into one of the traditional tort pigeon-holes, it is outlawed without further ado. It seems to me that the greatest obstacle to realistic decision-making is reliance upon precedent. Yet, after all, precedent is the style of the common law. May it be, then, that the courts will never be able to respond to the challenge of moulding the common law to changed circumstances and policies, absent clear legislative instructions?

Personally, I am not reassured by the brave words of an Ontario judge in a recent case. In granting, for the first time, an anticipatory or *quia timet* injunction, he remarked:

> I have not been cited any cases in which a *quia timet* injunction has been granted in labour matters nor have I been able to find any authorities myself. However, problems presented by new situations or by strange concatenations of circumstances have never been found insuperable by the law and, indeed, the genius of the common law has always been that remedy should follow need and that formalism never stultify justice. Nor, as has been said can equity be prescribed to be beyond the age of child-bearing.[14]

One good judgment deserves another. I can state my reservations no better than did that great American jurist, Mr. Justice Brandeis:

> The unwritten law possesses capacity for growth; and has often satisfied new demands for justice by invoking analogies or by expanding a rule or principle. This process has been in the main wisely applied and should not be discontinued. Where the problem is relatively simple, as it is apt to be when private interests only are involved, it generally proves adequate. But with the increasing complexity of society, the public interest tends to become omnipresent; and the problems presented by new demands for justice cease to be simple. Then the creation or recognition by courts of a new private right may work serious injury to the general public, unless the boundaries of the right are definitely established and wisely guarded. In order to reconcile the new private right with the public interest, it may be necessary to prescribe limitations and rules for its enjoyment; and also to provide administrative machinery for enforcing the rules. It is largely for this reason that, in the effort to meet the many new demands for justice incident to a rapidly changing civilization, resort to legislation has latterly been had with increasing frequency.[15]

In labour matters, Brandeis' prophecy of fifty years ago has proved sound. Today, Canadian labour tribunals exercise broad

[14]*Foundation Co.* v. *McGloin* (1964), 42 D.L.R. 2d 209 at p. 211 (per Stewart J.).

[15]*International News Service* v. *Associated Press* (1918), 248 U.S. 215 at p. 262.

remedial jurisdiction: simple and non-enforceable declarations, orders of reinstatement and compensation, elaborate and potent remedies such as cease and desist orders, and orders to dissolve a dominated labour organization.

So long as the men who administer these tribunals are competent and dedicated men, and so long as their procedures are fair, within the limitations of fast-moving problems, I see no objection to this trend. However, I am afraid many well-intentioned but poorly-informed lawyers possess an exaggerated and wholly unwarranted faith in the judges as creative lawmakers and as the sole guardians of due process. Their crusading zeal may yet subvert and destroy the immensely successful administrative tribunals which have grown up over the past half-century.

II

I turn now from my contemplation of our jurisprudential navel to the challenges posed by the irresistible social forces in the world around us, a world I have platitudinously described as undergoing a "revolution of expectations." One obvious symptom of this revolution is the increasing frequency with which society intervenes in disputes which are said to affect the public interest.

By any definition, I suppose, disputes in public utilities, in transportation systems, and in hospitals would fall within the ambit of the public interest. In each of these fields, the public has intervened in Canada in recent years, through legislation to forestall strikes by substituting a process of compulsory arbitration. How broadly should we define the public interest? Where does this intervention end? The United States government appears to have become an uninvited camel in the collective-bargaining tent of the American steel industry, gradually nudging the parties from the privacy of their conference room, into the hard cold light of public scrutiny, gradually substituting for labour-management consensus a government-coerced decree. Closer to home the strikes several years ago of the Royal York Hotel, and last year of the Toronto newspapers, were generally viewed as community crises. In both cases government intervened, once successfully, once unsuccessfully. But it is important to note that the legal framework of bargaining remains unresponsive to this challenge, except where community consensus is overwhelming, as in the case of public utilities, hospitals, and railways. Even here we have not responded with the imagination and flexibility that the problem deserves. Assuming that we wish to solve such disputes, if we can, by a process of collective bargaining, then it is evident that any statutory solution ought to maximize the pressures for bargaining, while safeguarding the public against the potential harmful results of a breakdown in negotiations. Instead, we have simply substituted arbitration for strikes, and we have thereby seriously impaired the calibre of collective bargaining. Indeed, there is every reason to believe that with arbitration as its terminal point, bargaining, as we know it in industry generally, will cease to exist in these special situations. Might it not be preferable to introduce an element of uncertainty, of flexibility, into the settlement of these disputes, in order to preserve some of the vitality of the bargaining process? I have in mind, for example, the Slichter Law in Massachusetts[16] which provides a choice of procedures in situations where industrial disputes threaten the public interest. While most of these procedures have their counterpart in one Canadian statute or another, I am not aware that the full range is available under any single Act. Of course, in the sense that *ad hoc* legislation, rather than pre-established procedures, has been the Canadian approach, technically the government of the day has an unlimited choice of procedures. But *ad hoc* legislation does have two disadvantages: it cannot quickly be enacted, and it brands one party with a stigma of irresponsibility which further inhibits bargaining.

A problem of broader dimensions, but lesser intensity, is that of technological or corporate change during the lifetime of the collective agreement. Sometimes, an employer may make such changes expressly in order to subvert the bargaining relationship. Sometimes, the changes are normal responses to competitive pressures. Has the law really proved capable of

[16]Mass. Stat. c. 150B, s. 2, as am. by L. 1947, c. 596.

adjusting these clashing interests—the desire for industrial relations stability and the need for managerial flexibility in a competitive economy? Let me take as an example the successor rights problem. It is no secret that some employers have engaged in a form of corporate metamorphosis for the express purpose of shedding their collective-bargaining obligations. Particularly in industries such as construction, where the good-will attaching to a small construction firm is negligible, might an employer conveniently go out of business and emerge under a new corporate charter. In so doing, under the Labour Board's jurisprudence, he was able to rid himself of the union which had organized his employees. The Goldenberg Royal Commission recognized that this device promoted industrial strife and had no apparent compensating benefit to the industry as a whole. Accordingly, the Commission recommended amending legislation, which ultimately was enacted. Whether or not the legislation adopted in Ontario, Manitoba, British Columbia, and other Canadian jurisdictions is really adequate to the task at hand is a matter of serious controversy. It is noteworthy, however, that the National Labour Relations Board in the United States, unlike our own labour boards, solved the same problems without legislative assistance.

The related problem of subcontracting has also been met with a singular lack of imagination and intellectual sophistication by Canadian arbitrators. Again without regard to a contrary American jurisprudence of substantial dimensions, the trend of the Canadian law has been to permit subcontracting wherever the work is no longer to be done under the employer's supervision and direction. Adopting a highly irrelevant test of employment from the law of agency, and prostrating themselves before the doctrine of management rights, Canadian arbitrators have failed to appreciate the potential risks of subcontracting to industrial peace. Similarly, the runaway plant problem has evoked a minimal response from our legislators and labour boards. The issue is by no means clear, but I suggest that a balance must be struck at some point between an employer's absolute freedom and the interests of his workers and their union. Where the movement of work is the product of economic pressures, for example, a desire to be nearer markets, suppliers, or transportation, labour relations policies are no more than a neutral factor in evaluating it. It is rather humanitarian concern for employees displaced or left behind which may prompt public intervention. However, where dislocation or plant removal is motivated by anti-union sentiment, our public policy of promoting collective bargaining has been thwarted. The runaway plant, or the plant that has displaced its workers to escape unions, is certainly falling below a community standard of conduct as surely as the plant which pollutes a nearby river or produces a nuisance in a residential neighbourhood. Although control may be difficult, given a "rule of reason" it should not be impossible to ensure compliance with community standards.

Allied to the problem of allocating work between those in the bargaining unit and those beyond it is the problem of allocating work between men and machines. A collective-bargaining contract constructs an edifice of classifications and wages upon a foundation of stable and familiar techniques of production. Particularly in mature and sophisticated collective-bargaining relationships do the parties evaluate carefully the labour content of jobs, to ensure that remuneration will correspond to effort and skill. Moreover, the seniority clause does not merely protect the older worker for humanitarian reasons; it assumes as well that the senior employee will be more highly skilled and thus better qualified to fill highly paid jobs. This latter assumption is also based upon the continued existence of familiar production patterns. Finally, the very premise of collective bargaining itself assumes a stable rather than a dynamic need for labour; it is the predicted availability of work or the anticipated effect of a threatened withdrawal of services that ultimately pressures the parties to bring about an agreement during their negotiations. Technological change may shatter this foundation of assumptions and topple the entire legal edifice.

Consider the impact of technological change on the wage and classification structure. The agreement identifies by name a number of jobs. If their content is radically transformed, or their very existence ceases, what wages and classifications are then to apply to the former occupants of those jobs? To foresee all new classifications which might conceivably come into existence during the lifetime of the agreement is an obvious exercise in futility. To forbid the introduction of new machines (and thus of new job classifications) is to place an impossibly high premium on stability, with almost disastrous consequences for the employer's competitive position. Yet to allow the employer freedom to break down old work patterns is not to say that he must be allowed freedom to erect new ones. If the employer could simply establish new classifications, he might destroy the fruits of collective bargaining by his unilateral act. By and large, neither the parties nor the law have responded in an imaginative fashion to the challenge of reconciling the employer's freedom to innovate with the regime of collective bargaining. Unions have asked for the right to strike to force the employer to agree upon new classifications and wages. This right is now denied to them by reason of the statutory duty to arbitrate all disputes arising during the lifetime of a collective agreement. Employers are content with the *status quo*, because the statutory obligation to arbitrate only extends to disputes arising out of the interpretation or application of the agreement, and not to the fixing of new wages and working conditions. A compromise, one which appeals to me as a reasonable use of a legal mechanism, is to entrust the fixing of new terms of employment and wages to third party adjudication. This is not to say that such adjudication must in every case take place. Rather, the possibility of arbitration provides an incentive for the parties to resolve their differences by negotiation. I might be accused of inconsistency in stating that arbitration of wage disputes in public services impedes collective bargaining, while it has the opposite effect in disputes involving the reclassification of employees after technological change. But let me point out that in public service disputes there are potentially large gains to be had in arbitration which cannot be won in negotiation, so that one of the parties would rather arbitrate than negotiate; contrariwise, in classification disputes, the new wage rates an arbitrator will likely fix, which may often affect only a few employees, will be only marginally different from the former rates, so that there is an incentive to avoid the time and expense of arbitration. On this proposal, a single caveat: who will arbitrate? With no disrespect to my fellow arbitrators, few of them are skilled in job evaluation. Most people with experience and expertise in this field are employed by either unions or management and are consequently unable to act as neutral arbitrators. I would strongly suggest that the parties and the government together begin to consider a program of recruitment in this highly sensitive, and obviously expanding, area of labour arbitration.

A long-range solution for the problems of workers displaced through technological change does not ultimately lie either with collective-bargaining legislation or indeed with the collective-bargaining process. While the problem has its genesis in the employment relationship, it is obviously a larger social problem. The victims of technological displacement, particularly older workers who cannot adapt to new industrial techniques, represent in two senses a failure of society. In the first place, they are a failure of our educational system: we simply have not trained people to be adaptable. Secondly, they represent a failure of our social security system: we are not yet able to cope with the appearance on the labour market of that largely unmarketable commodity, the unskilled worker. We have not really learned to avoid human spoilage and waste. My position is that responsibility in this area lies beyond the narrow labour-management community. The burdens of training and retraining, of job-finding and job-making, cannot be borne by a particular company and union whose resources and horizons are necessarily limited.

The most fundamental impact of technological change has been upon the balance of power at the bargaining table. The brutal but inescapable reality of our newspaper strike is that the employer no longer needs to hire striking union members, or even unemployed non-union printers. Now the computer crosses the picket line and "scabs" in the struck plant. Deprived of the traditional technique of mounting economic pressures, the strike, it can fairly be expected that unions will experiment with other tactics. Some of these are so obviously anti-social that they cannot be permitted. Desperate attempts to stop the circulation of newspapers by destroying them, or physically obstructing their delivery, now appear to have been abandoned, as much I am sure because of the good sense of the strikers as to the vigilance of the police department. Let me pause here to note that the law's response to violence or to the destruction of property is predictable and usually effective because there is such wide social agreement on the undesirability of such conduct. A much more acceptable tactic, one much closer to the mainstream of industrial combat, has been the exertion of various forms of secondary economic pressure. Attempts have been made to persuade readers not to buy newspapers, to persuade merchants not to advertise, and to persuade non-striking employees to cease work. All have some arguable validity in a situation where the mere withdrawal of labour, the standard bargaining tactic, has virtually no impact. Yet in each attempt, the strikers have been confronted with legal obstacles, some legislative, others judge-made. While the law has been inept in resolving the underlying dispute, it has certainly helped to determine the outcome of the strike by preventing various forms of economic pressure. On the one hand, it is possible to simply shrug and say that the printers are in the same position as any weak union, and had best accept the realities of that position. On the other hand, this counsel of despair is an admission of the willingness to contemplate the ultimate breakdown of collective bargaining, as we know it, in many areas of industry. However, the law could be changed to permit the union to launch countervailing pressures which would to some extent offset the advantages of the computer. In other words we might shift the contest from the labour market, where it is no longer meaningful, to the consumer market where the parties are more evenly matched, by making legal certain forms of secondary pressure which are not now permitted. More realistically, I suspect that unions will be able to redress the balance of power not by changing the law, but by altering their structure so as to embrace a wider range of employees, not all of whom would be pitted against the computer in competition for work. Thus, in the newspaper industry, an industry-wide union, whose members gather news as well as print it, would not have been subject to the same pressures as the much more narrowly-based craft union.

This last observation brings me to a critical theme. Is it possible—or desirable—to reshape the union movement by compulsion of law to meet the revolutions of our times? Again, by way of example, I focus upon the revolution of expectations. More and more we are coming to expect of our union movement a level of responsibility, integrity, democracy, and social consciousness, which would make it an institutional refutation of the doctrine of original sin. Can the law guarantee our expectations? Obviously, legislation can do much to stop overt forms of undesirable behaviour. The Landrum-Griffin Act in the United States, with its Bill of Rights for union members, makes legally enforceable the right to democracy and honesty in union administration. In response to a much less urgent situation, a number of scattered provisions have appeared in Canadian labour legislation which seek the same end. Overt forms of racial and religious discrimination, recently forbidden in the United States, have for many years been outlawed in Canada.

What I am concerned to trace here is not the undeniable fact that law may have some influence, but a more precise analysis of exactly what that influence is. Obviously, law acts as a deterrent. Yet equally important is the educative role of law; by a public declaration of the standards of conduct which we expect, many will be led into voluntary, indeed willing, compliance. As a sage has remarked, "many a man has become a good man by leading a life of hypocrisy." Thus, by continually doing what is expected of us, even without a deep belief in the conventional morality, we may gradually come to believe in its validity. On the other hand, there is no denying the fact that even the most vigorous program of enforcement cannot overcome widespread public indifference or hostility to the law's objectives. The prohibition era proved this. Thus, it is important that any law directed towards shaping the destiny of the labour movement be enacted with the assistance and participation of those most directly concerned. I believe that the vast majority of our labour leaders are firmly committed to democracy and honesty, and they ought to be invited to help make laws which would apply to the tiny minority that are not. Because there is a natural and justifiable fear that those outside the house of labour do not always possess a sympathetic understanding of its tenants, so far as possible the enforcement of such laws should also be an internal matter. The Public Review Board of the United Automobile Workers is an excellent model of non-governmental, union-created machinery which can and should be utilized in any systematic approach to regulating the internal affairs of labour unions.

But when we turn from the more obvious dangers of "boss-ism" to the much subtler questions of union structure and organization, law may well be too crude an instrument to accomplish our purposes. For example, Parliament has imposed a trusteeship upon the Seafarers' International Union and the other maritime unions, which has not brought the ultimate in organizational purity but has at least curbed the worst abuses of power. The trusteeship has been totally unable to execute its task of welding the various maritime unions into a single effective organization. Moreover, even in the internal reform of the S.I.U., the trusteeship has been compelled to acknowledge institutional realities and loyalties, which have combined to perpetuate in office most of the officials of the Banks' era. I do not mean to suggest that government is powerless to control one of the most important private institutions in our society. Rather, my point is that government must operate not so much by command as by example and exhortation. Consider, for instance, the way in which a more highly centralized union movement might be promoted. By constantly involving the various central labour bodies in economic forecasting, legislative revision, and consultation in policy planning, the importance of these central bodies *vis-à-vis* their affiliates is greatly enhanced. Industry-wide bargaining likewise emphasizes the authority of central labour bodies. Therefore, when government itself bargains, it clearly ought to insist on centralized, rather than autonomous, union negotiators on the other side of the table. And when collective bargaining takes place in the normal way between employers and unions, government leadership can give great impetus to industry-wide negotiations. That the attempt in the Ontario construction industry, following the Goldenberg Commission Report, to conduct such negotiations under government auspices was unsuccessful should not foreclose the experiment for all time. But I wish to emphasize that, in my view, a law which compels the dissolution or merger of unions, which compels their affiliation or non-affiliation with national or international groups, is an unwarranted interference with a basic civil liberty—freedom of association—which would not seem to be justified by any labour relations crisis in the recent past or present.

III

I shall conclude, on the theme with which I began and upon which I have touched several times throughout my remarks: by what process of law-making can legal institutions and rules be made to respond more quickly and effectively to the challenges of industrial relations? In my view, this is a crucial question, for it is the way in which law is made, as much as its content, that determines its effectiveness.

I make no apologies for seeking my answer in the experience of Scandinavia, an experience that has been characterized by a high degree of success, by a deep commitment to democracy, and by frequent experimentation to meet the changing demands of the industrial environment. The key to law-making in Scandinavia is the full and active participation of labour and management. Characteristically, legislation is passed at the joint request of the parties, to implement policies agreed upon between them. An active role in the administration of legislation is assigned to the labour and management federations. Often, indeed, their consensus makes legislation unnecessary, and they live under a form of private self-government. What I propose is that we import from Scandinavia this central, sensible concept of labour and management participation in the process of law-making. To secure this participation I urge the establishment of a labour law commission, a sort of industrial parliament, in which would be gathered unionists and businessmen, lawmakers, and academics. Its concern would be an ongoing examination of existing policies, a reasoned exploration of new proposals, and outspoken support for legislation and institutions which intelligent men of good faith could accept as the reasonable compromise between divergent interests. I use the term "parliament" fully aware of its double connotation. The French word *parlement* originally described a chamber of discussion. Indeed, some would say that this description is equally apt today. I intend that this labour law commission should be a chamber of discussion. At the moment, there is no neutral ground upon which labour, management, public officials, and the academic community can meet regularly. There are no occasions, beyond the crises produced by collective bargaining, or controversial legislative proposals, for the exchange of views. Thus, there is no accumulation of a fund of goodwill that stems from familiarity and respect, upon which the parties may draw in difficult times. I think, therefore, that there is much to be said for a chamber of discussion. But "parliament" in our contemporary sense is a legislative body as well. In a special way, I should hope that this industrial parliament would also legislate. Naturally, I do not mean for a moment that it should usurp the functions of the duly elected legislators. However, I would expect that a measure which had been carefully examined, and approved, by such a representative body would have no problem in mustering the necessary parliamentary majority. Once enacted, moreover, laws would more effectively command the obedience of all concerned, because of the pre-commitment to legislative policy by well-known unionists, business leaders, and disinterested critics. As well, I would hope that the industrial parliament could give the kind of expert and detailed attention to legislation which is so difficult to obtain within the machinery of government. For this purpose, I would hope that the industrial parliament might be supported by a civil service of economists, lawyers, sociologists, industrial management consultants, and labour staff members, recruited and mobilized by the universities.

Finally, and perhaps in the far distant future, I can envisage voluntary adherence by labour and management to the standards of behaviour enunciated by the industrial parliament. In securing this voluntary adherence, the pre-eminence of the representative members would be of obvious importance.

I conclude by quoting the remarks of Professor Archibald Cox, until recently Solicitor-General of the United States. In a remarkable speech entitled "Lawyers and Social Ferment" Professor Cox said:

Even in a time of ferment and necessary social change—especially in such a time—the most important thing about the legal profession is that we inherit the tradition of seven or eight centuries of continuous concern for the institutions and aspirations—for the processes, ideals and sense of right and justice—that make for free and civilized society. . . . Our own era has urgent need for lawyers not to resist change but to channel the vital forces at work in the community along the lines of justice and reason, on a scale and at a pace heretofore unprecedented. Only thus can we fulfil our ancient heritage. . . . [17]

As a lawyer, then, a member of a profession centuries old, and as a student of industrial relations, a discipline whose existence can hardly be measured in decades, I can ask for no more than a vital interaction between the law and the industrial relations community. I hope that each will work its magic upon the other, so that the older discipline will be rejuvenated, and the younger brought to maturity.

[17]Address to Hastings College of Law, University of California, reprinted in (1965) *Harvard Law School Bulletin* 6.

PART III

ON THE FRONTIER OF INDUSTRIAL RELATIONS

6

The Individual
in an Organizational Society*

WILBERT E. MOORE†

IT IS UNDOUBTEDLY PERVERSE of me to suggest that we may be out of phase, but I sincerely believe that the field of "industrial relations" as we have understood the subject in the last three decades does not have much of a future. I think most of the subject matter of the field has been misunderstood, misconstrued, and misrepresented by both the academic community and the staff representatives of industrial relations in business and industry. The academics and the practising professionals have shared in a kind of conspiracy. The conspiracy consists in a mutually reinforced will to believe in a myth: the notion that the concept of industrial relations is precisely definitive of a singular and crucial division of the industrial labour force. The argument runs thus: between management and labour there is a great gulf fixed. Each party is homogeneous, organized, and articulate. And since these parties are caught in a condition of coerced co-operation, they have relations. But I suggest that this gulf has not been very firm or very fixed

*I owe the term "organizational society" to Professor John William Ward, now of Amherst, who several years ago conducted a Princeton University Conference on the theme.
†Russell Sage Foundation.

since the latter part of the nineteenth century, when the corporate structure started to emerge, and has been even more fluid ever since.

While most management men and the newly emergent spokesmen for labour interests were accepting the Marxist notion that there was a fundamental division between property owners and the people in their employ, the bases of proprietorship were shifting. Managers have become proletarians by strict Marxist definition. Workers have been steadily upgraded rather than downgraded in average educational and skill levels. A growing proportion of white-collar workers could not be called managers, nor production workers, nor clerical record keepers and communicators, but rather technical, scientific, and professional workers. The whole traditional fabric of industrial relations has come apart at the seams, and indeed has shredded into tangled strands. Specialized occupational interests, division by rank, by function, by bureaucratic subdivision, and highly individual preoccupations abound in the contemporary work organization. The industrial relations man for management is also a professional, and thus already in a role-conflict situation. He is supposed to deal with hard-bargaining unions, whose united front is increasingly rare. Life is now complicated, and it will not get simpler. *Au contraire*, he may find himself bargaining for himself and his peers almost at the same time that he is bargaining against other representative, collective interests. If we mean to take the term, and the scholarly mission of "industrial relations" seriously, we must surely attend to contemporary organizational complexities, and not assume that we are dealing with two well-organized antagonists. I shall return to the industrial setting in due course, but first I want to take a somewhat broader view of what organized life means to the individual participant in contemporary civilization.

Paradoxes abound in contemporary society. We are becoming simultaneously more specialized and differentiated in our ways of making a living and in our life styles, and more homogeneous in our basic consumer standards and participation in the national culture. We are becoming increasingly committed to the nuclear family consisting of parents and their immature children, with generations and adult siblings and spatially separated, and increasingly reliant on communications and informal transfers of services among the nominally separate units.

I offer here another paradox, though its character is partially semantic. We are both disorganized and highly organized, and indexes of both would undoubtedly show an upward slope through time. Many of the phenomena of daily life in the United States and other contemporary societies that are identified in the popular press or in sociological texts as examples of social disorganization are genuinely pathological. That is, the conditions or actions so identified reveal failures of the society to fulfil stated aims, or threaten its capacity for continuous operation, or at the least demonstrate that some segments of the population enclosed in the society's political boundaries have somehow not performed according to normal expectations. Despite some tedious attempts of occasional sociologists to identify every action or social manifestation as subtly beneficial to the social order, I think it should be said plainly that some social behaviour is clearly sinful or otherwise disruptive. Most of crime and delinquency and of various indicators of alienation, such as alcoholism and drug addiction, can be taken as displaying the failures of social organization. On a grander scale occasional manifestations of discord merit the designation of disorganization. I refer, for example, to truculent polarization in political allegiances, such as the unconscionable pretentions to virtue on the part of persons who have unmerited privileges, or the dismaying displays of discontent among those who have succeeded beyond their dreams as well as, plainly, beyond their merits. The radical left when it had some significance often offered a certain appeal to equity, while offering silly or iniquitous schemes for its achievement. The radical right does not even offer equity, but only the restoration of a mythical, heroic past when people knew their place.

Yet there are certain examples of disorganization that are such only by comparison with an abstract—I will not say ideal—model of a perfectly integrated system. By this view, we may look at a society cross-sectionally—that is, at a moment of time—and observe widespread differences in custom and cuisine, in residence and religion, in economic interest and political intent, in belief and behaviour. Competition and discord meet the eye, and the elementary facts are not changed by calling the system pluralistic. With a little more trouble, we can also observe unequal rates of change in various aspects of social phenomena. If they all fitted together neatly once upon a time, that has not been true lately, and will not be in any future that matters to mortal men.

Though some of the disorder, both persistent and changeful, that meets the observer's eye is truly random or aberrant, a great deal of it is organized. And that brings me back to the paradox that while the indexes of disorganization increase, so do the indexes of organization. In terms of concrete aggregations of individuals with common goals and regular procedures, of collective forms of working and playing, of disciplined procedures for pursuing the production of goods or the exchange of information or the governing of men, human concerns do get organized. Not to join the group is to be a social isolate, and that is social death.

In the real world of experience, the closest approximation to the integrated complex society must necessarily be the totalitarian structure, where inconsistency, competition, and choice are at least nominally forbidden, and where all change is nominally planned and directed according to a grand scheme of temporal priorities and necessary functional counterparts.

If, therefore, I here adopt the position of the social critic as well as that of the social analyst, it is within the context of preserving pluralism, with all the untidiness that is the cost of permitting a measure of liberty and therefore choice, and not that of suggesting an insufferably tidy system.

Before dealing with such grand themes as the position of the modern American corporation, and problems of responsibility and power in big business or big government, I want to ease into the subject by looking at some of the other organized features of contemporary society.

LET'S GET ORGANIZED

"Now is the time for all good men to come to the aid of their party." Untold millions of student typists have printed out these words, most often thoughtlessly. The call to organize, to join in collective efforts, is heard throughout the land, and it seems that it grows louder as competing voices contribute to the din.

Freedom of organization and assembly is a cherished political right in Anglo-American legal systems. Though the legal environment is more restrictive where codified law prevails, as in Western Europe, and associations are highly manipulated in communist countries, all modern societies display a plethora of organizations. Many of these associations have little to do with the work place or the residential community, though some may have their primary locus and rationale in occupational and community life.

For convenience, associations may be divided into two categories: interest-oriented and expressive.[1] Interest groups are organized to do good or at least to combat evil. The common interests of their members may be occupational—labour unions and professional societies come to mind—or otherwise economic. Thus, local merchants banded together as a chamber of commerce may seek new industry for the community, causing a counter-organization of residential property-owners adjacent to the proposed industrial site. Incidentally, since American political parties represent coalitions of heterogeneous interests, the issues that divide local communities rarely cut along party lines; the constituted political machinery accordingly proves inadequate for resolving the problems and new, essentially political, organizations are created *ad hoc*.

Interest groups often represent the narrowly selfish concerns of the members. Such groups tend to preclusive membership: ". . . only a spy or a pretty silly joiner would become identified with two or more contestants."[2] The group is likely

---

[1]See Wilbert E. Moore, *Man, Time, and Society* (New York: Wiley, 1963), chap. 6, "Voluntary Associations."
[2]*Ibid.*, p. 107.

to be viewed by its members as a mere instrumentality for making common cause among those with like concerns, though some organizers and high participators may indeed become committed to the collective identity as such.

Of course not all interests are selfish in the ordinary sense. Charitable and welfare associations also appear, and make their claims to allegiance. They compete with amateur sporting clubs, groups devoted to the more passive recreation offered by bridge or poker, and a host of literary and collectors' societies. These expressive associations are not commonly and overtly divisive, as are the narrowly constituted interest groups, but in the States the array of American associations of both types offers ample testimony to the intrusion of racial and ethnic distinctions into matters ranging from technical occupations to butterfly collecting that appear to have little relevance to ethnicity.[3]

The association may be defined residually as a formally constituted organization representing the like or common interests of members, for whom membership does not constitute a livelihood. Some large associations do afford paid staffs, but this administrative detail scarcely affects the fact that associations are essentially non-work organizations. Indeed I have argued in a recent book[4] that associations are to be found primarily in modern industrial societies whose work organizations are also highly specialized and where there is a fairly sharp demarcation between mandatory time—represented by the school and the job—and discretionary time.

The groups we have been discussing are often called voluntary associations, for in the pure case—which may be closely approximated only in the Anglo-American institutional system—the individual has the option of which associations he will join, and in fact whether he will join any. Occupational associations commonly attempt to achieve mandatory monopolies over practitioners, with varying degrees of success, and even organized charity can be compulsory if it uses the evil

[3]See Frederick G. Ruffner, Jr., *et al.*, eds., *Encyclopedia of Associations*, 4th ed., vol. I, *National Organizations of the United States*. (Detroit: Gale Research, 1964).

[4]Moore, *Man, Time, and Society*, p. 104.

offices of employers to coerce participation. But there is also a subtler problem of freedom in a highly organized world. Does one any longer have the rational right not to join? Self-help may be inadequate in pursuit or protection of one's interest if those with adverse interests gain strength through collective action. Another typing exercise goes, "The quick brown fox jumped over the lazy dog," and its moral in this connection is that the right to apathy may have been lost irretrievably.

THE PERILS OF PLURALISM

The performance of everything from the world's work to the world's play by functionally specialized organizations presents the individual with problems that are usually discussed in terms of status and role. There are problems of status consistency when the individual is a participant in many distinct contexts of action, in each of which he is subject to formal ranking or at least to evaluation of performance. There are problems of role conflict when organizations enter competing claims on time, treasure, or emotional allegiance on the fractionated individual, who must still somehow attempt to act as an integrated entity.

But functional specialization may also be viewed in terms of inter-group relations. Specialization, we have seen, by no means insures against competition for scarce resources. Even where there is clear complementarity among the specialized units—the family and the factory, the service club and the church, the union and the bowling team—there are ample opportunities for conflict, especially in terms of power and jurisdiction. It is merely tedious to note that groups as such do not feel, plan, or act; individuals do these things on behalf of collectivities. Inter-group conflict cannot be understood at the individual level.

The necessity of dealing with groups becomes self-evident when they do not share a common membership, when, in fact, membership is preclusive. Even when there is complementarity between the preclusive units—for example, physicians and nurses, business management and labour unions, manufacturers and retailers—the opportunities for conflict remain. Indeed, they may be heightened by struggles for power and jurisdiction in carrying out their interdependent functions.

Other preclusive groups may attempt to become "totalitarian," to establish separate and largely self-contained communities. Historically the communitarian sects tried to set themselves apart from the world. And in the urban setting settlements of recent immigrants maintained a separate identity that was a joint product of poverty, discrimination, and choice. Both types of separateness were subject to the intrusive effects of larger forces: the commodity market, the labour market, the state, and its perhaps most devastating instrument, the compulsory public school.

Though various sectarian and ethnic groups have become "assimilated" in varying degrees and at varying speeds, assimilation cannot be understood solely in terms of the sacrificing of old beliefs and customs in favour of a unified and dominant culture. The dominant culture has incorporated the traits of ethnic minorities while incorporating their carriers into the social life of American society.

Yet ethnicity is by no means a thing of the past, and in the conspicuous case of the American Negro is very much with us indeed. Yet despite the exceptionally submerged status of the Negro, the dominant culture itself is strongly marked and enriched by elements of Negro origin.

The American language, polity, and economy have evolved while mainly retaining their course with relatively minor effects from the diversity of religious and ethnic elements. Religious diversity persists and is an outstanding feature of American pluralism. Political diversity persists and incorporates ethnic interests, but ethnic and racial interests are rarely decisive at the national level. On all these scores the Canadian situation is more complex.

To counter the homogeneity feared by critics of mass culture, we have been considering some strongly competitive and even divisive elements in the contemporary scene. Cuisine, art styles, and religious beliefs have become matters of preference, tolerable differences rarely leading to organized hostilities. Ethnic conflict in the United States now involves only Negroes and Puerto Ricans. Economic interests and political views command the capacity to stir passions and occasionally to imperil public order and the interests of third parties. But perhaps the greatest perils of pluralism come not so much from frontal oppositions but from such a degree of discretionary specialization that a common identity or a common culture is lost to a host of diverse organizational interests. The other side of tolerance is indifference, and that may go to the point of disengagement.

BUREAUCRACY RAMPANT

We have so far avoided the workaday world, which now deserves our attention. Here especially we are organized, possibly to a fault. The economy of individual farmers, craftsmen, and traders was in good part fictional when it was made the model for classical economics early in the nineteenth century. The magnitude of the myth has increased ever since, as larger and larger proportions of the labour force are co-ordinated, not primarily by the market but by the authority of owners and managers. A simple measure of bureaucratization is the proportion of the labour force composed of wage and salary earners, leaving out independent farmers, individual proprietors, and those professionals and craftsmen in what we may call private practice. This proportion is highly correlated with indexes of economic development as countries are compared at a particular time, and has grown more or less steadily in the older industrial countries.[5] In the United States, over four-fifths of the labour force is bureaucratized by our definition, and farming is no more immune to the process than is urban manufacturing or governmental service.

The problems posed by bureaucratization are generally so well known as to require no more than brief recapitulation. The solutions to the problems are less easily called to mind, for some of them do not exist.

One of the first problems to be noted is that, despite our

[5]See Wilbert E. Moore, "Changing Occupational Structures," in Seymour Martin Lipset and Neil J. Smelser, eds., *Social Structure and Social Mobility in Economic Development* (Chicago: Aldine, 1966).

cherished ideology of individualism, most members of the labour force have bosses. The realization that most of the bosses have bosses in turn may soften the subordination by sharing it, but that is not likely to help much. The employed individual is constrained by authority but also by a complex division of labour that requires highly specialized performance. Though the narrowness of specialization may decrease as one moves to higher levels of skill and authority, the progression is neither regular nor certain. Many relatively well-paid bureaucrats, public and private, are almost as completely "boxed in" as is the man whose actions are paced by a machine.

By organizing work—the producing of goods, managing money, providing public services, healing the sick, or educating the young—through complex and interdependent administrative structures, we gain the benefits of specialization in higher productivity, and pay certain costs. We separate work in time and place from most other meaningful activities of life, and at the workplace itself we threaten man's initiative and occasionally even his dignity. The "organization man"[6] is depicted, with partial accuracy, as subjected to demands for conformity —to the stultification of creativity. For many, a stable career consists of relatively passive rides on up-bound escalators rather than climbing the ladder,[7] though at higher altitudes an occassional executive finds himself airborne in an ejection seat.

I do not want to paint too dark or too monochromatic a picture. For many factory workers, technology has passed beyond the phase of human subordination to mechanical requirements and pacing. The remaining workmen manipulate and monitor machines, or else diagnose their ills and apply therapy. Some managers have opportunities for being venturesome, if their prior experience has not systematically suppressed their creative abilities. And a rapidly growing, though

[6]See William H. Whyte, Jr., *The Organization Man* (New York: Simon and Schuster, 1956).

[7]See Wilbert E. Moore, *The Conduct of the Corporation*, (New York: Random House, 1962), chap. xii, "Climbers, Riders, Treaders."

still small, proportion of organizational positions demands truly professional qualifications and perforce offers indulgence of the professional's typical commitment to creative problem-solving. In fact, it is the increase in the demand for specialized and rapidly up-dated knowledge and the use of that knowledge for rational decision that prevents bureaucracies from being too rigidly authoritarian. The manager often knows less than his subordinates, each in his own field, and that situation has a moderating influence on the exercise of power.

The individual has some other protections against the massive power or massive inertia of organizations, but all of them in combination may still be an inadequate foundation of freedom. First, though the individual employed by an organization thereby submits himself to terms and conditions of work that are in the first instance administratively determined, he has not, in most instances, totally abandoned the protection of the market. Where the individual is not free to change employers, as he is not in totalitarian regimes or in military service, his subordination to the system lacks this elementary protection. An employers' association blacklist has a similar consequence. And it sometimes happens that the individual's accumulated experience is so peculiar to a single employer's operations that there is no effective external market; he can move only by losing some of his skill and therefore market value.

Second, the individual may have collective protection through labour unions or other occupational associations. The effectiveness of such organized protection depends upon the capacity of the employee's organization to hold an effective monopoly on the services in question and thus to prevent the employer from substituting more amenable workers for the recalcitrant objectors. Such a capacity in turn necessarily rests upon political protection of employee organizations; the state becomes an invisible third party to disputes if it does not actually become a visible one. It should be underscored that it is not only manual labourers or department store clerks who have such organized protection. Professions commonly seek licensing from the state as a way of maintaining standards, and many make actual membership in the professional association an additional condition for practice. But this means that the salaried professional is always protected by his brethren, at least implicitly, particulary against demands that he perform contrary to the established codes of his calling. Note also the irony that the individual gains some independence from the employing organization by submitting himself to the discipline of another organization. The union or professional association, however, offers at least the nominal forms of democratic determination, and that is clearly not the case with administrative regulations set by bureaucracies.

A third and rarer protection is provided by an independent judiciary for the adjudication of disputes in such private polities as corporations or universities. We may note that judicial processes are built into military organizations, where the individual lacks the protection of the market, and many civil service systems have orderly bases of appeal. Though civil service appeals often involve job security, the military court offers one way of dealing with another problem intrinsic to bureaucracies: the abuse of power. How does the subordinate avoid compliance with an "illegal" order, that is, one contrary to the established rules and precedents of the organization? Union contracts often provide for a multi-stage grievance procedure which is essentially judicial, but the managerial employee commonly lacks such protection, except that a one-stage appeal to the boss's boss may prevail as a more or less formal right. Until business management becomes truly professional in both technical and ethical standards, and that is some considerable way into the future, there is a fairly strong case to be made for judicial procedures in private bureaucracies.

There is, fourth, another alternative to the internal judiciary, and that is the legislative and judicial protection of the state itself. We have now established fairly extensive precedents for legislative action on wages, hours, safety and workmen's compensation, the rights and powers of unions, and so on. There is also some precedent, but less firmly established, for review by the regular courts of the abuse of administrative power. One way of doing this in our legal system is to view the announced administrative regulations of private organizations as constituting contractual conditions for all employees. This is the principal basis in law and equity for firing the subordinate who fails to do his job or violates various rules. But what happens when principal officers violate rules, or middle managers violate rules out of sight of their superiors but at the expense of their subordinates? Who guards the guardians? In most private corporations, they guard themselves; a notoriously flimsy restraint on the abuse of power. It is in this area where I think we may expect to see a rise of external review if private organizations do not take steps to provide their own restraints.

THE UNTIDY SOCIETY

Although everywhere we look we encounter multiplying organizations, some of which are growing in size and power, the total result is remarkably disorderly. The meaning of freedom is choice and the cost of choice is uncertainty, but we cannot so glibly gloss over some glaring defects of the contemporary disorder.

Take first, the giant corporation.[8] It is by no means free of restraints, but it retains substantial powers of irresponsible action. The market offers some discipline, but consumers may have at least as great a dependence on one of a strictly limited number of suppliers as the converse; and if those suppliers act in concert, even if implicitly and without illegal conspiracy, the consumer has little protection. The corporation also has other clienteles: stockholders and other investors, suppliers of materials and components, employees, local plant communities, the state in its multiform activities, and the public not elsewhere classified. But the restraints and interests bearing on the corporation often work at cross-purposes, and require balancing, placating, or even manipulating. These and other duties fall on the chief executives, and the very confusion of interests

[8]The paragraphs on corporate responsibility are based on *Ibid.*, esp. chap. I, "Management in Moral Crisis," and chap. XXI, "Public: Political and Profane."

and uncertainties about goals warns us that we cannot be sure how all this chaos gets organized. Stockholders are treated as another clientele, neither irrelevant nor clearly primary. The quest for position in the market appears to account for corporate behaviour better than the quest for profits. And there are strong signs that the organization itself, and particularly its managerial inhabitants, take top priority among the interests that corporations serve.

Self-interest is not despicable in our traditions, particularly in economic activities, as long as there are counter-balancing restraints to protect the interest of others. And that is where the contemporary conduct of the corporation appears to me to be weakest. In sociological language, the large corporation with diversified equity ownership is incompletely institutionalized, as the older restraints of private property and competitive markets have not been replaced by more relevant responsibilities. To say that corporate managers have now become trustees of their organizations to assure their continuity and their current service to clienteles is to substitute one uncertainty for another. The responsibilities of trusteeship are also poorly defined in law. But one qualification of the trustee is firmly institutionalized, and that is that his service be disinterested. The richly rewarded corporate executives clearly fail that crucial test. To say that corporate managers are becoming professionalized, with what that implies by way of intellectual and ethical standards, represents a small measure of truth, but the process is very incomplete and its completion still would not resolve the issues regarding the priorities among clienteles, or to put it another way, the answer to the question, what is the corporation for?

Having turned over one batch of uncertainties, let me consider another aspect of pluralistic organization. Though we speak of self-service—which is essentially passing on part of distribution labour to the consumer—man is irretrievably social and most services are rendered for others. In fact, viewed precisely, all labour consists of services, but so do other acts for the benefit of others. If we ask, how do services get performed and allocated in human societies, the most frequent answer would be in terms of kinship and related structures and various informal but traditional reciprocities within communities. Within modernized societies there are two other modes of getting services performed, and in some still a third. One of the major marks of modernization is the development of a labour market, which means in effect that services are rewarded with wages, salaries, or fees. Some of these services are devoted to producing and distributing physical goods, but others are devoted to administration, to education, and indeed to ministering to all man's concerns from the religious through physical and psychological health, relations to the law, and to such mundane matters of traditional concern as care of those too young, too feeble, or too old to care for themselves.

In all modernized societies the market mechanism for getting such services performed is supplemented, and in some virtually supplanted, by the intervention of the state. Rather than various benefits being contingent on ability to pay, they are rendered on the basis of "need" by public agencies. Thus the "fisc" is substituted for the market, with taxation based on ability to pay, but no guarantee of a *quid pro quo*. Indeed, the mechanism is precisely that of a "transfer" from those who pay taxes to those who need services, with virtually every adult in both categories in one respect or another. It is a mode of distribution that has received remarkably little intelligent analysis from the scholarly community, as economists are rather uneasy outside the market mechanism, and other social scientists have lacked the skills or the interest in dealing with the ways welfare benefits are handled. While their hearts bleed, their minds lack the vital juices for thought.

We have in the United States, not uniquely but to an unparalleled degree, another alternative to informal, market, and fiscal modes of providing services. That way is private philanthropy. I should like to call this a "fourth force." This is not the time or the place to drag out numbers and balance sheets, but it is evident that both the charitable organization dependent on current contributions and the endowed charitable trust play extremely important roles in scientific research, health, education, and miscellaneous welfare activities including the fine arts along with nursery schools as examples of welfare.

In this area, once more, we encounter the problem of trusteeship, but not terribly tainted with the crude calculus of self-interest. Not that we can assume that all chairmen of community fund drives, or workers in voluntary social work agencies, or the professional staffs in endowed foundations are self-abnegating saints, but rather that they are under more severe lawful restraints and not subject to such ambiguous definitions of their situation as being possible beneficiaries of rewards for having a good year in the market. About the only external review of the responsibilities of foundations comes from an examination of their tax exemption, but it is surely high time that some more dispassionate scrutiny be given to their appropriate functions in an organizational society that provides alternative mechanisms for private benefits and public well-being.

I have viewed my mission here as pointing to some unmistakable trends in the shape of our modern era, with several sharp glances at uncertainties that call for mature consideration and possible action. I do not plead for a system that is tidy, for that way lies total constraint and possibly collective disaster. But I do think that it is not too much to ask that some social scientists develop a sense of relevance that need not destroy their claim to objectivity. The relevance I have in mind includes examination of the alternative ways of solving life's dilemmas and the intrinsic problems of organized existence, some of which grow in urgency and all of which change in their realistic manifestations. We have increasingly turned to government, and national government at that, for resolving conflicts and curing glaring inequities. Most of the alternatives so far offered are plainly reactionary: a nostalgic reconstruction of a mythical past which was in fact unmistakably evil. The powers now at our command are greater, along with the problems they pose. Organize we must, and legislate we must, and adjudicate we must—for these are standard mechanisms for problem-solving and tension-management. But underlying these is the necessity to understand, to identify, and, let it be said plainly, to set goals and preferences. It is just possible that an organizational society that is pluralistic can survive. But not without good sense along with good will.

7

Government and Poverty

THE HONOURABLE MAURICE SAUVÉ°

WITH THE RISE OF AFFLUENCE in our society, we have developed programs of social insurance and social security which ensure that all, or nearly all, of the population have at least a basic minimum of the necessities of life—food, clothing, shelter, and elementary medical care. Some would deny, therefore, that poverty exists in Canada because, by traditional definition, the condition of poverty is the lack of the basic requirements of life. However, according to the standards of our society, people may be considered poor even though their income provides much more than these basic necessities. If, for any reason, people are prevented from enjoying a reasonable level of security, comfort, and amenities, they are considered poor. And since our society is generally humane as well as affluent, poverty has become a matter of political concern.

It is not, I think, that the poor generally believe their condition to be a direct responsibility of society; we are too steeped in the philosophy of individual free enterprise for that. It is that their champions recognize that the condition of the poor is now, in this era of automation, attributable to the maladjustment of socio-economic organizations. It is these

°Minister of Forestry, Government of Canada, Ottawa.

theorists, these disturbers of the "conventional wisdom," who act as the conscience of society and thus—in an increasingly direct and forthright way—influence politicians.

In Canada, politicians have, in the past few years, responded to the point of accepting this new "political" definition of poverty and have committed themselves—probably irrevocably —to a large-scale reduction of poverty thus defined. No one should be surprised to find this a principal concern of politicians and political parties during the next decade or two. Let me now comment, as a politician, on the problems that may face those who become involved in this new challenge—the challenge of poverty. Because my experience to date has been largely with the Agricultural Rehabilitation and Development Act, I may allude to rural poverty more often than to urban poverty, but I trust that my generalizations will prove applicable to urban as well as rural areas.

The condition of poverty is not a simple condition. It is not attributable to simple causes, although the moralist can always proclaim a quick and easy answer, derived from a naive folk belief of our society, that hard work and virtue are inevitably rewarded. Parenthetically I must make it quite clear that I am not opposed to hard work and virtue, but I do not believe that poverty necessarily stems from lack of them. Poverty has many facets, some found in the macro-economic framework, some found in the broad cultural setting, some found in the local *mores*, some found in the level of social capital available, some found in the relative productivity of the natural resources, some found in temporary or permanent dislocations caused by shifts in technology or demand. More particularly, poverty is linked to low intelligence, lack of education, ill health, and, as is often the case, to ill fortune. One could go on for some time elaborating on the many factors which alone or in combination may create a condition of poverty. It is enough to say, however, that from our knowledge and experience there is substantial evidence that poverty is many-faceted and complex.

Before going on to discuss the implications of this fact in terms of government programs, I should like to describe poverty in real, substantive terms as it existed in rural Canada in 1965. Early that year, the Department of Forestry, through its ARDA Administration, commissioned a study on rural poverty. The study was done by the Canadian Welfare Council and included actual case studies of poverty in four regions of Canada—one in Nova Scotia, one in Quebec, one in Ontario, and one in Manitoba. It was a pilot study, and not a particularly large and elaborate one, but it was done by competent people and their descriptions of what they found are objective. I will attempt in as concise a way as possible to acquaint you with the findings of this study—to sketch poverty as it actually is, here and now, in Canada.

The typical poor family in these four rural areas consists of parents and five children. The father works at a combination of self-employment—it may be a bit of farming, fishing, or woodswork—and part-time wage employment. The income is in many instances supplemented by welfare payments or unemployment insurance in addition to the family allowance. Even with this, the per capita monthly income is $28. We might note that the assumption underlying the minimum wage is that about $50 is a necessary monthly per capita income.

The housing conditions of these families are described as poor in the majority of cases. Many of them lack running water and have no inside toilet facilities; foundations, if they exist, are faulty; windows are broken or lacking; the roof leaks; there is no insulation. One not unusual illustration describes a house, built in 1964, of used planks and old wood retrieved by the head of the household from the dump. In this house everybody, and there are eight children in addition to the parents, sleeps in one finished room.

Opportunities for the children in these families are poor. Medical care is either expensive, too far away, or the facilities are inadequate. Educational facilities, while present, are in many cases deficient. Full participation in the educational process is hampered by such seeming trivialities as lack of clothing, no place to do homework, no books at home, and fatigue associated with poor food. Occupational opportunities are limited partly by inadequate education and training and partly because jobs are not available. Parents see little or no future for their children in their home areas. Such jobs as are available are often seasonal and wages are low. The capital requirements of modern farming are prohibitive for persons whose expenditures, in seven out of ten cases, exceed their incomes.

On the whole, these families have little in the way of recreation other than television, perhaps, and visiting with any neighbours close at hand. They are not members of the formal social organizations in the community and have no voice in decision-making groups such as local government. Although they are interested in school and church affairs, they find it difficult to participate in them.

These families exhibit a courage one must admire in facing conditions which they see no possibility of changing. It is not that they do not wish to change but they find no realistic possibility of doing so. Some have tried and have failed. Their skills, their orientation towards how things should be done, and their lack of experience in coping with urban industrial situations trap them in a socio-economic dead-end.

In defining their poverty, these families place emphasis on the concrete difficulties they have to face. This is reflected in such definitions as "to be poor is to wash one's clothing without soap." They recognize their lack of opportunities to a greater degree than do the community leaders who are often tempted to attribute poverty solely to individual causes such as laziness, mismanagement, or lack of ambition. It is not lack of ambition that recognizes the inevitability of accepting a low-paying job when one has no training. It is not laziness which keeps members of poor families working long hours at hard manual labour. And if one's income is less than is needed in order to live, is it mismanagement to get in debt?

It is a picture of people no different from ourselves in moral character. They are of many origins, young and old, healthy and ill. At present, most of them do not despair but they fear for the future of their children. Forces of social change and decisions made by others have placed these families, to a deplorable extent, outside the benefits of modern life.

This is not a pleasant picture of the lives of a large group of the citizens of four areas of Canada. And the broader statistics available on poverty indicate clearly that such conditions are found in greater or lesser degree nearly everywhere in urban and rural Canada. The conditions of rural poverty and these broad statistics seem to indicate that the gross national product is far from being the barometer of national well-being. If, in our humane and relatively well-ordered society, such conditions can exist, I take it as an ominous indication that we have lagged dangerously in our ability to evaluate and assess the implications of the technological powers now in our possession. The modern tragedy of poverty lies beyond the pain and suffering it brings to the individual. It is, I believe, that though we have fashioned the technological instruments to conquer this age-old anguish, we have not yet mastered the use of these techniques to reach that objective.

Following from this, and keeping in mind that poverty is a many-faceted condition, I wish now to discuss a serious flaw in governmental organization in this area. I believe that there is a weakness in the execution of government programs aimed at reduction or elimination of poverty in Canada, a weakness which seems to frustrate our attempts to directly face the challenge of poverty and take effective action. One could define this weakness broadly as an incapacity to understand and communicate understanding, a failure to transmit information and receive a "feedback" response to this information. But, this sounds a little high-flown when one attempts to relate it to the condition of a marginal farmer, obsolete and old at fifty-five, who has no reason for hope. Therefore, I shall attempt a more modest and pragmatic exposition of the flaws that I sense in our governmental organization for "anti-poverty" programs.

We face a peculiar conundrum. It is politically safe, even politically desirable, to wage a massive frontal attack on poverty. We have the productive capacity and the financial means of doing so. Almost no skilled men are unemployed. We have an able and responsible civil service, both at federal and provincial levels. The census of Canada, the great surveys of natural resources, and thousands of individual research programs, both rural and urban, provide us with nearly all the information we need. Why in this situation does poverty persist?

Certainly no one with any real knowledge of Canadians in the low-income category could seriously contend that the poor remain poor because they are lazy, or because they are irresponsible. Such a conclusion could be based only on most superficial or cynical observation, and certainly it is not confirmed by research reports such as the Canadian Welfare Council study which I have described to you.

It is the politicians who define the wants of their constituents in such a fashion that the civil servants may organize the administrative programs required to fill these wants. It has been the case in recent years that politicians have defined in broad terms the objective of combatting the condition of poverty. The many branches of the federal and provincial civil services have responded with what resources were made available to them, and have conscientiously tried to adapt these resources and capabilities to meet the challenge of poverty. It is possible to make a very impressive list of the results of these programs; however, we know they have been, at best, only partially successful. And the evidence of this is the fact that many hundreds of thousands of families still exist in a condition of poverty.

Why is this? Why is it that honest and sincere efforts, backed by considerable expenditures, have not resulted in a greater reduction of poverty in Canada? There is no simple answer to this question. In fact, we all know there are many answers. But I feel bound to try and identify the weakness which I said I had sensed in government programs. And I know as I do this that there is a risk of appearing to oversimplify.

The present organization and structure of the civil service has evolved as a group of many hundreds of individual agencies, and each agency has limited, specialized functions. Thus each agency can relate its activities to only a limited facet of the life of any given citizen. Each agency seeks to make citizens conscious of its function, and to do this it may publish information in various forms, and make personal contact with citizens. But let me stress again that the individual agency of modern government deals with only a small facet of the day-to-day life of any citizen. This means simply that if a citizen is to have maximum benefit from government programs, he must be familiar, to some degree at least, with a considerable number of programs. This is not an impossible task for the well-educated, alert, and well-informed middle class particularly since their direct needs from government are quite limited. But what about the poor people of the country? They need a great deal from numerous government agencies; yet most of them are not in a position to establish a functioning relationship with these agencies. The reasons for this vary from illiteracy and physical isolation to social isolation and language barriers.

There is also another more general reason. The government agencies are oriented to commodities, to sectors of economic activity. They are oriented as well to increasing productivity, and if they spend too much of their time trying to help people who cannot produce for one reason or another, the agency may look inefficient. For example, the job of the agricultural representative is to help increase farm production. Two hours spent with a well-equipped, well-capitalized farmer may help that farmer increase his production by several hundred dollars per year. On the other hand, two hours spent with a poor, ill-equipped farmer may have little or no effect, because the basic means of production at his disposal are deficient. Which farmer is an agriculture representative likely to pay most attention to—the man who can apply his advice easily or the man who can apply it only with great difficulty?

It would be easy enough to cite many examples of such dilemmas if one examined all the programs of the federal and provincial governments. And this, in my opinion, is the basic weakness of our government organizations when they seek to enable the poor to enter the productive economic life of our nation. The fact is—and it is an unfortunate fact—that communication between the governments and the poor is extremely difficult. Somehow, there must be built a communications bridge between those who are in need and those who have the power to help them. Without such a bridge, the complex condition of poverty cannot be grappled with effectively by the kind of administrative structure we have developed in this country. Its absence, I believe, has been the fundamental weakness of our attack plan against the enemy of poverty.

What kind of a communications bridge should we develop? Once again, there are many avenues and many roads to our objective. One could say that improved formal education would be a useful part of the structure. One could say that improved public information methods of government agencies would be useful—and who can deny that there is room for clear and lucid statements which can be easily understood by most of the people? The number and capability of field men could be improved, no doubt. But it is doubtful that, even if we very greatly improve all that we now do, this would, in fact, establish the required interaction between governments and low-income people.

In order to become successful in our society, the poor must change, and most of them wish to change. But change in people and their social institutions can occur only through actual involvement and experience. What we are faced with is this: that while some kinds of change can be brought about by edict of government, lasting, and constructive social change cannot. Change in individuals and social institutions emerges from a consensus of new expectations. New expectations are not very tangible, however. They are rooted in people's minds as beliefs or ideas concerning what should be. While new expectations may be suggested by administrative programs, they become active only when they become accepted in the minds of people generally, and thus come to constitute working parts of people's attitudes and opinions. Such changes are brought about, as we are increasingly aware, not by imposition of government programs, not by edict, but through the direct experience and involvement of the people. *Both* government programs and the involvement of local low-income people are necessary if the challenge of poverty is to be met. Where programs to eliminate poverty have failed, or have not been fully successful, the failure can be traced to this crucial absence of communication.

Is there a general solution to this problem?—a solution which is compatible with the fairly rigid administrative structures we have evolved; a solution which is philosophically acceptable to a democratic free-enterprise society? I feel that there may be, and that this solution is to be found in a social process which is relatively new, but which has been developed with success in many communities in many areas of the world both under-developed and developed. The name given to this process is "community development"—a name that has come to have a precise meaning when it is used by the specialists who have come to understand and apply community development as a social process. The term "community development" has come to connote, "The processes by which efforts of the people themselves are united with those of governmental authorities to improve the economic, social and cultural conditions of communities, to integrate these communities into the life of the nation, and to enable them to contribute fully to national progress." The definition then points out that the essential element of this complex process is the participation of the people themselves, and the provision of services in ways which will encourage initiative, self-help, and mutual help.

This, of course, is not an easy process to establish because it can be easy for a government representative to mishandle a relationship with a community. One pitfall is authoritarianism or paternalism. Another is the tendency to spread propaganda and build the expectations of a community beyond what can be attained. A further pitfall is that the community itself may seek to exploit the anti-poverty program by organizing to grab from the pork barrel which it may assume exists. In short, people who seek to introduce the community development process must be extremely sensitive and intelligently aware of the social forces which operate even in the simplest rural community. This means that their personal qualities, education, and training must be of the highest order. To develop and employ this kind of person will require substantial training facilities and substantial salary levels.

There are certain positive steps which those of us who seek to build the bridge between the Canadian institutions and the Canadian poor can begin taking. First, we must recognize that effective contact is not being made with this segment of the people. Second, we must recognize that contact is essential before useful development can occur. Third, we must recognize that until the low-income groups are assisted in arriving at some consensus, and in more or less formalizing their demands, we can do little. A fourth point is that governments, both federal and provincial, should consider seriously taking a bold step in committing substantial resources to this new community development approach. Community development is admittedly new and it is admittedly relatively untried in Canada, and the approach is certainly not an easy one for the government administrator to build his action programs around. Yet it may prove to be the only way to develop successful anti-poverty programs, and for this reason I feel it is urgent that it be given the understanding and support of governments.

I would like to return briefly to the program which is a particular responsibility of mine—the Agricultural Rehabilitation and Development Act. As you know, the ARDA legislation was passed in 1961 to expand the area of opportunity available to the very considerable segment of the rural population which has been unable to benefit from the general growth of the economy, and which has, in hundreds of thousands of instances, sunk lower in the economic and social scale of this country. The ARDA legislation implied the assumption of federal responsibility for rural income levels, but it did not imply that this responsibility carried with it the prerogative of federal intrusion into provincial planning and implementation in the management of natural resources or in the social and economic development of rural areas. ARDA is a federal-provincial program, in which the provinces initiate, implement, and administer projects and programs. The role of the federal government is to share costs, provide some forms of technical assistance when required, and do some research. An important but not clearly defined role of the federal government is to function as a clearing house for information and to work towards improving co-ordination among the scores of participating agencies—federal, provincial, and non-governmental.

I will not at this time go into the details of the ARDA program as it has developed, except to say that it has evolved into a substantial program of resource improvement and rural socio-economic development. The federal government is enabled to contribute 125 million dollars towards provincial ARDA programs during the next five years. The point which I do wish to make about ARDA is this: the ARDA concept and program is unique in Canada in that it seeks, by practical programs and other measures, to overcome those weaknesses inherent in our administrative institutions to which I alluded at some length earlier. The approach of the ARDA program might be described as "holistic," in that the fragmentation of government agency effort can, to some degree, be compensated for by positive measures for improved co-ordination. It is a program which, unlike most others, can be geared to the problem of the whole human being in his rural environment, not merely to one facet of the individual's life nor one limited sector of his environment.

A number of examples could be mentioned of various areas in Canada where ARDA programs are developing according to this broad, "global" concept of socio-economic development. May I briefly refer to the program in one region—the Lower St. Lawrence and Magdalen Islands. The Gaspé Peninsula makes up most of this area which has depended mainly on forestry, fisheries, and agriculture for its economy. Incomes are now extremely low. Under the ARDA program, the Eastern Québec Planning Bureau—le Bureau d'Aménagement de l'Est du Québec—was incorporated in 1963 as a non-profit organization. It is financed in equal proportions by the federal and provincial governments. This organization, which we refer to as the BAEQ, is concerned with research and the planning of development programs. The research program is very comprehensive, and it is intended that the programs and projects will be equally comprehensive.

The most original part of this major experiment in regional development is seen in the way in which the BAEQ and the people of the region are making contact and communicating with each other. This process could be called community development within the definition I gave earlier. Locally, in the Lower St. Lawrence region, it is called *l'animation sociale*. During 1964 about 225 local committees were formed so that participants might express their views about the problems of their localities and the solutions to these problems. *L'animation sociale* in this region can already be given credit for worthwhile work. To name only one accomplishment there has been outstanding success in getting adults interested in further schooling; 5,000 adults have registered for instruction in 235 adult education classes, and some local groups are continuing their study. One must recognize that there are many difficulties yet to be solved, in research, planning, and developing worthwhile programs for this region. However, the successes to date, here and in several other regions of Canada, indicate that the community development process can indeed produce results.

No doubt the ARDA program is not ideally perfect; however, I do say that it has emerged as one of the most successful ventures to date in the area of federal-provincial action. I am greatly optimistic that the ARDA program will, as it develops, help our Canadian institutions to overcome the very real organizational obstacles to coping with the challenge of poverty.

8

War on Poverty

TOM COSGROVE*

RECENT FIGURES released in the United States show a decline of about a million in the nation's poverty population. Those of us who have been fighting the war on poverty welcome these figures. We are not so naive, however, that we attribute the gain to the present anti-poverty program alone. We know that much of what has been accomplished is attributable to the massive prosperity our nation has been enjoying. We have been enjoying a 6 per cent growth rate for nearly two years. There is no need to be an economist to understand the implications of such growth. Despite automation, unemployment is down in the face of record demand. Incomes have been rising and, in such a situation, it is inevitable that some among the poor will escape poverty's bonds.

The *Wall Street Journal* of September 27, 1965 carried a lead article applauding the results of the present economic boom in the United States. It reported that despite the entry into the labour market of maturing postwar babies, there is reason to hope that joblessness will drop to 4 per cent by this year's end. Yet, even if today's great prosperity continues indefinitely, there will be massive poverty south of the

*Executive Secretary, Labour Advisory Council, Office of Economic Opportunity, Washington.

forty-ninth parallel unless it is fought unceasingly. By the official statistics, any family earning below $3,100 per annum is poverty-stricken. On the basis of such statistics, there are perhaps 34,000,000 impoverished residents in the United States.

Mollie Orshansky, an economist for the U.S. Social Security Administration, has drawn a somewhat different profile of poverty. Her profile includes some 50 million Americans living within the shadow of poverty. However poverty is defined, there is no getting away from the ugly paradox of needless want in the face of the greatest plenty any nation has ever accumulated. So long as any citizen of the United States suffers needless privation, the great American dream will remain unfulfilled.

Contrary to much popular belief, the overwhelming majority (about 78 per cent) of the poor are white, although poverty is twice as prevalent among non-whites. Poverty stalks the Negro city ghetto, the back streets of the inner city where poor whites cluster, the Indian reservation, and rural America. Of the poor, some 54 per cent live in cities, 30 per cent live in rural areas, and 16 per cent live on the land. Over 40 per cent of farm families are poor by American standards.

The poor of the United States are better off than a majority of the world's population. Some, perhaps, are not poor by Canadian standards, although I note that your own definition of poverty is not far different from ours. The point is that in a world dominated by want, poverty is a relative concept. Relative though it may be, poverty in the United States must be defined against the background in which it exists, and the same is true for poverty in Canada. Because such poverty exists side by side with such great wealth, it is especially bitter to those who taste it each day of their lives.

Poverty takes many different forms. In the United States, a third of poor families include persons past age 65. Loss of earning power because of age is a major factor contributing to poverty. Millions of Americans depend solely upon social security income in old age, despite the growth of private pension plans. Congress recently increased social security benefits by 7 per cent, but the average is still under $90 monthly.

A myth exists about the laziness of the poor, which deserves to be buried for all time. The very people who spread this myth often pay paupers' wages to domestics and others in service industries. Often, those who shout loudest of the unworthiness of the poor are those who fight improved minimum wage legislation. The statistics prove that the poor want to work, although there are some too demoralized or alienated for self-help. Those who would condemn these unfortunates truly condemn only their own insensitivity and indifference. While the lunatic right may proclaim that the poor should be left in poverty, most American citizens support the anti-poverty war.

More than half of all poor families in the United States include members who are working or looking for work; about two-thirds include wage earners who worked at least part of the time during the year. It is the poor who perform the stoop labour in the fields, who clean away the dishes in fancy restaurants, who make the beds in our hotels and motels, and who perform so many of the other unskilled tasks that still must be done. More than half of all poverty is attributable to low wages, involuntary unemployment, and involuntary part-time work.

Sooner or later, the affluent American society must squarely face up to the problem created by the one-parent household. Most of these homes are headed by women. Often, they contain young children. Regardless of the cause—whether death of the male head of the house, disability, or desertion—the mother cannot obtain employment at wages that will permit adequate child care while she is at work. Often, it is more economic for society to have this mother remain at home to rear the children than to work. Some day, perhaps, our wealthy United States may begin to understand that rearing children under these circumstances must be a full-time paid job. A new kind of culture seems to be developing in the Negro ghetto where the one-parent family is common. Children often grow up without the presence of a male in the household. The mother is the sole expression of parental authority; the masculine role is down-graded. The male child, in turn, loses conviction concerning his work and place. In the ultimate, American society will be called upon to pay a still higher bill for its failure to make normal life possible.

The Ontario Federation of Labour study entitled, "Poverty in Ontario, 1964," contains the serious charge that, aside from a limited study in New Brunswick, "there has been no serious attempt made by the authorities to assess the nature and depth of poverty" in Canada. Within the study is very familiar language:

> Because poverty breeds poverty, it is self perpetuating. Children of poor parents are most likely to be poor themselves because their parents are usually unable to give them the needed education, health, or, in many cases, the incentive to improve their lot. Low family income, poor housing with its accompanying frustrations, and the resulting environment are not favourable for bringing up a new generation that will play a constructive role in our society.

The cycle of poverty is hardly unique to Ontario. It has existed for generations within the United States. Its results are sometimes fearful. It has created apathy and dependence. It has caused frightening crime and delinquency. The recent riots in the Watts area of Los Angeles attest to the bitterness and violence pent up in the impoverished Negro ghettos. Figures cited by the Ontario Federation show that about four million Canadians live in either poverty or destitution. Percentagewise, Canadian poverty is much the same as that to the South. As in the United States, poverty is greatest among minority groups—in your case, the Indians. As in the United States, poverty is often traceable to unemployment or underemployment. As with us, many of your poor work at substandard wages, are untrained or undereducated, or head one-parent families.

The war on poverty in the United States is an effort to break the poverty cycle, to help the poor to help themselves, to mobilize national and local community resources to eradicate the causes of poverty, and to equip the poor for the labour market.

Some claim that people are poor because they lack education. Others claim that people lack education because they are poor. But it matters not which comes first; it matters only that opportunity for education, training, and jobs shall be increased so that ignorance and want can be eradicated.

The entire nation has a stake in the eradication of poverty, because its existence is a threat to everybody's welfare. The poverty-stricken buy few consumer goods or homes. They add little to the national wealth. The elimination of poverty, obviously, means greater prosperity for all. Poverty is bad morality and worse economics.

As an American trade unionist, I support the war wholeheartedly. As a trade unionist, I urge a broader effort. I feel that the war on poverty must be won on the economic as well as the welfare front. I do not feel, for example, that education and training are major answers for poverty in old age. The answer, obviously, is adequate retirement income. The Auto Workers Union and the Steelworkers in recent contract settlements eliminated the fear of poverty in old age for tens of thousands of workers by negotiating more adequate pensions for retired members.

I could take the narrow view that the answer to elimination of poverty in old age lies through union organization. To an extent, this is true. But union organization will not answer the problem for millions. The answer lies in allocation of sufficient resources to assure a decent minimum living standard under social security. The United States can move further in this direction. Its economy now is approaching a $700 billion level. President Johnson has pointed out that we shall have a trillion dollar economy within two decades. Certainly, want in old age can be abolished in such an affluent society. Up to now, we have relied upon payroll taxes to finance social security improvement. The time has come, however, to turn a new corner and finance part of costs from general tax revenues.

The U.S. Economic Opportunity Act is consistent with President Johnson's belief in the value of education and training, and the need to place special emphasis upon our children and youth. The EOA declares that it is the "policy of the United States to eliminate the paradox of poverty in the midst of plenty." It proposes to open to all "the opportunity for education and training, the opportunity for work, and the opportunity to live in decency and dignity." This historic statement represents a more than passive welfareism since it proposes an active role for those to whom the commitment is made.

The United States first undertook a commitment to an active manpower policy with enactment of the Employment Act of 1946. This Act pledged maximum employment consistent with price stability. It was, in effect, a pledge that the federal power would be used to prevent major cyclical deflations and runaway inflation. For many years, the emphasis was upon fear of inflation. But in 1962, Congress enacted the Manpower Development and Training Act, which marked the start of an active manpower program in the nation. The Economic Opportunity Act extends this policy, although it is far more than a manpower program.

The Johnson anti-poverty program goes beyond the Economic Opportunity Act. The Elementary and Secondary School Act places stress upon assistance to schools teaching the children of the poor. The enactment of Medicare will largely eliminate fear of high medical care costs among the aged. The "opportunity scholarships" within the Higher Education Act, together with the work-study program originally included in the Economic Opportunity Act, will make it more possible for children of the poor to gain college education.

Organized labour in the United States has been a mainstay in the successful battle for recently enacted legislation. Labour, almost alone, carried on the fight for Medicare when the odds against it seemed insurmountable. Organized labour has had a major and positive role in the fight for civil rights and equal employment opportunity. There is a direct and obvious link between the civil rights fight and the war against poverty.

Partly because of high and persistent unemployment and partly because of the need to bring impoverished youth into the mainstream of our national life, the war on poverty has placed great stress upon youth programs. Unless young people are given an opportunity to overcome educational and training deficiencies, many will be condemned to repeat the cycle of poverty. The world no longer has adequate room for the high school drop-out or the unskilled who now are doomed to face lives of chronic unemployment and underemployment. Title 1 of the Economic Opportunity Act represents a conscious effort to provide impoverished youth with the background and motivation needed for today's world of work.

The best known and most publicized program is the Job Corps. This seeks to provide an away-from-home residential setting for disadvantaged youth who have family backgrounds that discourage education and training, and which create negative motivation. There are three kinds of job corps centres: rural men's conservation camps for those with low levels of literacy; urban centres for young men able to absorb skill training; and women's centres. Youth from sixteen to twenty-two are eligible. At full strength, there will be some 66,000 in the various camps and centres. Enrolment will be for a year in most cases, although some may go from conservation camps to job corps centres for additional training.

There have been problems at some job corps installations, some of which have been blown out of proportion. Several publicists and seekers after political advantage have implied that the program is in deep trouble. I reply now categorically that the reverse is true, although there have admittedly been problems. The Job Corps, like all EOA programs, is new, untried, and novel. Most of the youth enrolled come from seriously disadvantaged family situations. Many have never before been away from home; some have never experienced parental discipline; others lack personal hygiene habits; still others have suffered serious alienation. Yet the drop-out rate from the Job Corps is significantly lower than the first-year college drop-out rate in the United States. Further, there are signs that, with experience, initial problems are being solved. In my own mind, the Job Corps will make a significant contribution toward a better society in the United States.

The Neighborhood Youth Corps, another significant youth program, has been subjected only to minor criticism because it has already proven successful. The program seeks to make it possible for poor youth to remain in school through part-time work for pay, and to improve their employability in the process. It also seeks to encourage drop-outs to return to school or to obtain useful work experience.

What is true of the NYC is equally true of the College Work-Study Program, now being transferred to the federal Office of Education and enlarged considerably under the new Higher Education Act. Wages made possible by federal funds for part-time work will permit tens of thousands of poor youth to obtain a higher education.

Following the Second World War, the Congress of the United States enacted the GI Bill of Rights. This was an investment in human capital that has paid off very handsomely. It enabled tens of thousands of youthful returned veterans to go to college or take advanced skill training. Because of the GI Bill, which paid tuition and a small stipend, the United States today has people with the know-how needed for a modern technological society.

The time has come when we are awakening to the realities of our modern world at long last. The National City Bank of New York has hailed investment in education as being as essential as investment in capital goods. The war on poverty provides funds for basic adult literacy courses in communities across the nation. The program is aimed at the 11.5 million adults with less than a sixth-grade education. While literacy does not guarantee full citizenship participation, or employment, these are almost impossible to achieve without the ability to read and write. Illiteracy, in a sense, is as severe a handicap as blindness. In a sense, illiterates may be further shut off from our world than the blind who can read braille.

The war on poverty embodies an effort to fight rural poverty through an individual small-loan program and loans to create or strengthen rural co-operatives. Some 500,000 low income rural families are eligible for these loans. Additionally, the Office of Economic Opportunity provides a program of loans to provide better housing, sanitation, education, day care, and self-help for migrant and seasonal agricultural workers. There is also included within the program a special small business loans component intended to offer new opportunity to neighbourhood and other small businesses and to expand employment opportunity. This program provides a source of credit when all others are lacking. Loans are repayable over fifteen years or less.

The United States is sorely troubled by the hard-core adult unemployed who have lost their capacity to improve their situations unaided. To help meet this problem, an adult work-experience program has been developed. Congress has extended the scope of this program even beyond the President's initial request. The program seeks, among other things, to employ the hard-core unemployed on useful projects in the public interest in situations where they may develop or conserve good work habits, attitudes, and morale.

The Peace Corps concept first enunciated by the late President John F. Kennedy has been brought to the domestic scene in the United States by the War on Poverty. VISTA, Volunteers in Service to America, offers adult Americans from outside the poor population an opportunity to serve in the front lines in the anti-poverty war. VISTA now is capturing the imagination of the nation and there is reason to believe it will prove to be a highly effective force for progress.

The heart of the anti-poverty program, and its most controversial aspect, is the Community Action Program. This represents the hometown mobilization against poverty in neighbourhoods where the disease is rooted. Through CAP, EOA anti-poverty programs, and other federal programs having a relationship to the anti-poverty war, all joined together with local resources for common combat. Community action is not a substitute for existing welfare agencies, although it seeks to utilize these in a co-ordinated effort to combat the root causes of poverty. CAP adds new resources and innovation to the fight. Last summer, Project Headstart—our first massive pre-school venture—was successfully launched. There were some failures and some mistakes. But more than half a million tots benefited. Thanks to Headstart, preschool has already become a permanent feature in American education.

There have been charges that OEO and Congressional insistence upon participation of the poor in every level of employment and planning within the local CAPs is an assault upon the present political power structure. This is not the case, but there can be no doubt that the concept is bringing needed reforms and challenges and a new look at the needs of the impoverished population.

The involvement-of-the-poor concept has a parallel in labour organization. Although unions use professionals, the basic leadership is recruited from the shops. It is, indeed, at the shop level that most problems are solved. And it is from the articulation of shop leadership that unions learn the problems of the membership.

We have insisted that the poor shall be directly represented upon governing, planning, and advisory boards. More important, perhaps, is that we have insisted that the leadership of the poor shall have a place within CAP programs as neighbourhood workers and in other capacities. We look upon the program itself as an opportunity structure for the poor who have leadership capability but who have so far been submerged by circumstances beyond their control.

The Neighborhood Centers visualized by the CAP—and now in operation in most communities—are in a sense the local union halls of the program. Out of these centres, the neighbourhood workers recruited from the poor seek out those who need services provided by the program. We know now that the neighbourhood worker is the vital link between the program and the people. Without effective neighbourhood workers, CAP programs will tend to remain words.

Through the CAPs, we are developing day-care centres, remedial education, pre-school, manpower training and employment programs, health and vocational rehabilitation, housing and home management, legal aid, credit unions, and many other essential services. CAP, more than any other aspect of the war on poverty, represents an effort to eradicate the root causes of poverty. If, at times, it shakes up existing "establishments" or power structures, it is only because the poor are at last in motion.

We know, however, that although the programs have been doubled they alone will not end poverty. The United States of today can afford to underpin its economy with a minimum wage which will take all of the employed out of poverty. If, in a few cases, this means a slightly higher price, the affluent of our world can afford it. Better indeed that a head of lettuce sell for a penny more than that migrant children grow up in ignorance and ill health. Better, indeed, that the child of a laundry worker shall continue in school than that the cost of laundering a shirt shall be a penny or two less.

We know—and Congressional hearings have shown this to be true—that there need be no major alteration within the U.S. price structure as the cost of an adequate minimum wage. We know that the U.S. economy can grow at a continued fast pace if more purchasing power is supplied at the lower levels of our society. We know that poverty can be eliminated faster and more effectively through such steps than in any other way. We recognize that every aspect of the anti-poverty war will remain essential even if the minimum wage is pegged above the level of poverty.

There is a need to think clearly and boldly about the kind of economic underpinning required to conquer poverty. There is a crying need for national minimum standards of public assistance to ensure that no child shall go hungry or uneducated through no fault of his own.

Nor can the war on poverty be won if the worker is denied his fair share of our expanding economy. While it is a fine thing to be able to produce a record output of goods and services, that ability will become a mockery unless the goods and services are consumed. In the ultimate, rising living standards spur capital investment and create the jobs needed to permit people to rise out of poverty.

The AFL-CIO is co-operating fully in the struggle to end poverty. It has stated that "no war against want can be won without adequate family income protection for those who cannot be self-supporting." The Federation has called for job-creating measures to underpin the economy. Recent headlines about educational needs, air pollution, water pollution, the condition of our cities, and the "uglification" of our countryside attest to the requirements for work within the public sector. The Federation has termed it as a "sad irony" that the federal government of the United States collects $100 million in income taxes and $200 million in excises from the poor. Certainly, tax reform must begin at the bottom where the burden is too great to bear. Thanks to the AFL-CIO, the present minimum wage of

$1.25 per hour is paid to poor persons on youth and adult work experience programs. It is our belief also that job training should not be a device to subsidize employers who seek only a means to perpetuate poverty wages. We are for job training, indeed, but for jobs with meaningful horizons.

The AFL-CIO and many business organizations applaud the war on poverty and its programs. They have pledged full co-operation and they are providing it. They look upon the commitment of the President to eradicate poverty as one of the most important ever made by a civilized society.

Lightning Source UK Ltd.
Milton Keynes UK
UKHW012358200722
406167UK00001B/325

9 781442 639553